Enablers learned their unhealthy behavior as victims of a painful or difficult childhood. They typically grew up in dysfunctional families where they did not receive effective nurturing. As neglected children, future enablers learned that they got along best in this difficult and often dangerous situation by being caretakers and people-pleasers. They kept their own thoughts and wishes secret and put others' needs ahead of their own. They grew up confusing being *needed* with being *loved.* Sadly, they came to feel important only by being needed.

Enablers, as adults, often continue to consider themselves innocent victims who are making the best of a bad situation. Surrounded by crises, they "pull the family through" time and again. They are often seen as heroes by their friends. One of the most important points this book makes is that most enablers are *not* in their situations by accident. In adulthood, as Miller points out, enablers are volunteers rather than victims.

Miller offers us a refreshing and *hopeful* story. Daring to choose the more unknown and uncomfortable path of independence led her to a more *genuinely* loving family life and the self-respect she had never known.

From the foreword by
Jennifer P. Schneider, M.D.

THE ENABLER

*When Helping Harms
the Ones You Love*

Angelyn Miller

BALLANTINE BOOKS • NEW YORK

Hunter House Inc.
P.O. Box 847
Claremont, CA 91711

Library of Congress Catalog Card Number: 88-31993

ISBN 0-345-36848-7

This edition published by arrangement with Hunter House, Inc., Publishers.

Manufactured in the United States of America

First Ballantine Books Edition: October 1990
Fourth Printing: May 1992

Gift
M.D.

Contents

This book is dedicated to my family.

I wish to acknowledge those members of the psycho-therapeutic community who have shared their wisdom with me and encouraged me, over the years, to find my own answers. Most important, I wish to acknowledge my husband, who has had the courage to allow me to publish this book. If, at any time, he had asked me not to have it published, I would not have.

Foreword

The concept of enabling is now well known to addiction counselors and to members of Al-Anon and other self-help groups for families of addicts. Yet thousands of people who do not have an obvious problem with chemical dependency enable their spouses, children, and friends, without ever realizing that their "helpfulness" actually harms the people they love.

This informative book describes the effects of enabling behavior on a family in which no one drank alcohol. By sharing with us her experiences and the impact on her family of her changed attitudes, Angelyn Miller shows us that *enabling* is a much broader problem than is drug dependency. The concrete examples she gives of her own enabling behaviors demonstrate both how blatant and how insidious the problem can be. The courageous steps she takes toward recovering her own self-esteem and creating a healthy family life offer hope to all of us living in an enabling situation.

Miller was the devoted wife of a man who had recurrent episodes of depression and the mother of a son who had manic-depressive illness. Neither Miller nor her husband used alcohol, although both had alcoholic parents. For years she tried to smooth the way for her husband and son, while ignoring her own needs and wishes. Then one day she had a startling experience— when she uncharacteristically became angry and told her husband exactly what she thought of his moping around, his depressed behavior instantly improved. A similar incident with her son had the same result. She realized that although what she had said to them could have been considered cruel, her honesty had done more good than all her years of "toleration."

This insight led her to understand that when we prevent someone from experiencing the negative consequences of their behavior, we actually make it *comfortable* for them to continue being alcoholic, sexually addicted, chronically depressed, selfish, or dependent in some other way. In our misguided efforts to help, we deprive people of the motivation to change. They remain the same needy, dependent people with low self-esteem, and not the mature adults we think we are helping them to become.

Miller realized that her exaggerated acceptance of her family's weaknesses simply rewarded and encouraged those weaknesses. *It seems paradoxical, but the way we can best help the people in our lives is to give them the freedom to learn from their own mistakes.*

Enablers learned their unhealthy behavior as victims of a painful or difficult childhood. They typically grew up in dysfunctional families where they did not receive effective nurturing. This may have been because one parent was alcoholic and the other an enabler. There may have been a physical or mental illness in the family, or perhaps the parents were extremely busy or self-centered. As neglected children, future enablers learned that they got along best in this difficult and often dangerous situation by being caretakers and people-pleasers. They kept their own thoughts and wishes secret and put others' needs ahead of their own. They grew up confusing being *needed* with being *loved*. Sadly, they came to feel important only by being needed, so they chose a marriage partner who needed fixing.

Enablers, as adults, often continue to consider themselves innocent victims who are making the best of a bad situation. Surrounded by crises, they "pull the family through" time and again. They are often seen as heroes by their friends. One of the most important points this book makes is that most enablers are *not* in their situations by accident. In adulthood, as Miller points out, enablers are volunteers rather than victims. In order to feel needed, they choose, although not consciously, to become involved in problematic situations.

Al-Anon meetings are full of people who had an alcoholic parent and have been married more than once to an alcoholic. Women who leave a philandering spouse often find themselves attracted to another man with a wandering eye. In my own recovery, I came to realize that my philandering husband was just the last in a long line of emotionally unavailable men with whom I had had relationships. I had to take some responsibility for having chosen him as a marriage partner. And as Miller explains, when couples separate without dealing with their problematic assumptions, they will only find themselves in the same type of unhealthy relationship with a different partner.

As long as they are needed, enablers feel secure; should their partner actually become more independent—that is, *healthy*—their fear of abandonment can become overwhelming. Enablers may actually sabotage their partners' recovery in order to continue being needed. Miller offers us a refreshing and *hopeful* story.

Daring to choose the more unknown and uncomfortable path of independence led her to a more *genuinely* loving family life and the self-respect she had never known.

This is a challenging book. The journey is not without its hazards. It may seem devastating to your self-image to realize that you are not in fact a victim but a volunteer, and that your efforts to help are in the long run doing harm. This realization, however, can open the door to new attitudes and behaviors on your part; these changes can have a dramatic impact on your own emotional health and on the behavior of those you love.

The process which the author suggests for self-improvement is very similar to the Twelve Steps of Alcoholics Anonymous (A.A.), which are listed on pages 90–91. She also includes written exercises to help overcome enabling behavior, and recommends professional therapy. She advises attendance at Al-Anon if you are enabling an alcoholic. The Twelve Steps of A.A. and its affiliated programs are useful to *any* enabler, as Miller points out. If you are an enabler, I urge you to attend the A.A. group appropriate for your situation.

Professional counseling can help, too—whether individual therapy, family therapy, or both. Look for a counselor who is comfortable working along with a Twelve Step program to help you in your recovery.

This book is an outstanding testimonial to the benefits that are possible when you recognize that you are an enabler and are willing to take steps to change your behavior. Read it, share it with your family and friends, and put it to good use.

JENNIFER P. SCHNEIDER, M.D.

Jennifer P. Schneider, M.D., Ph.D., author of *Back from Betrayal: Recovering from His Affairs*, is a physician, mother, and community leader in Tucson, Arizona. She writes and lectures extensively on co-dependency, co-addiction, and sexual addiction.

The Enabler

When not in check,
　I will:
　pick up your shoes
　　carry your pack
　　　pay your traffic ticket
　　　lie to your boss
　　　　do your homework
　　　　　remove rocks from your path
and strip you of the joy
　of saying, "I did it myself!"

Angelyn Miller

Prologue

DURING THE DIFFICULT years of my enabling, I knew that something was wrong. Life had not become what I had believed it would. As I watched my husband and children falter in life, one after another, I viewed the situation first with disbelief and then with panic.

When I married Stan in 1958, I wasn't worried about the future of my relationship with him. I had a degree in human development and family relations from a major university. When I had children—Tom, John, Nina, and Bud—I wasn't concerned about what would be required of me as a mother, because I was a credentialed elementary school teacher and knew about children. I should have been ready to be the ideal wife and mother. Indeed, I thought I would be. But my family life evolved through the years in such a way that nothing I had learned prepared me for what was to come. I moved into a life that was so different from my plans and my imaginings that it took me many years to sort it all out.

The only positive thing I can say about myself during that period is that I did recognize that we needed help.

And I—naturally, because I always did everything for everybody—sought that help.

I tried everything. I went to counseling, enrolled in EST training, attended Gestalt workshops, joined encounter groups and women's support groups, took assertiveness training and courses in transactional analysis and neuro-linguistic programming. I provided myself with an incredible amount of information about personal growth and family dynamics.

But however well armed with ideas I was, it took a series of tragic events to turn this theoretical knowledge into genuine understanding. This is the story of those events. I have written it in response to the frustration I felt at not readily finding an explanation for why our family was functioning poorly—when I needed it most. The myriad theories and techniques, which were sometimes contradictory, often only made the picture more obscure. I wanted to see us accurately, to understand what was happening to us. I wanted a coherent interpretation, a focused picture.

Because I thought I was so well trained to be a homemaker and because I came from a generation of women whose principal goal in life was to produce a successful family, I was stunned by the difficulties my family was having. I attributed them mostly to my husband, then to my children as they grew older. *It had never occurred to me that I was an equal contributor to our problems*.

When a counselor finally pointed me toward Janet Geringer Woititz's writings on co-dependence and adult children of alcoholics, I began to understand the dynamics of our family life and my role in it. The concept of "enabling" provided the insight I had been searching for. Later still, after I had worked through my own stages of understanding and devised a personal therapy, I came across the Twelve Steps of Alcoholics Anonymous and the complementary steps of Al-Anon. In essence, my process had been the same as the one suggested in the Twelve Steps.

My statement to the world, or to whomever will listen, is that *the alcoholic family does not have a monopoly on enablers or dependents*. There are a great number of people like myself whose principal way of relating to others is to assume their responsibilities.

Portrait of an Enabler

I WAS COUGHING and wheezing from the dust that was hanging in the air, but I had to finish cleaning the basement. The new owners were to move in the next day. The room was a moldy, musty mess, filled with an assortment of junk. There couldn't have been anything there worth more than a dollar or two. I felt like sweeping the whole lot out the door and setting a match to it.

I was so tired from these two weeks of moving that it seemed to take twice the normal effort just to keep my arms in motion. I picked up a mildewed schoolbook that had belonged to my son Tom, a very responsible eighteen year old who would be going to college in the fall. I threw it in the pile going to the dump.

My youngest son, Bud, who had just turned thirteen, was hefting boxes up the stairs and carting them across the backyard to John, who was loading the truck. John, just sixteen, was the huskiest of the three.

As Tom helped me move everything off the dirt floor and onto the slab of concrete by the entry, I saw that our belongings had multiplied far out of proportion to our years of living in this house. A good half of them didn't seem worthy of the move, but I continued to sort, throwing most things into the pile whose fate was questionable.

I was pleased that my sons had come with me to help. It wasn't voluntary, though. Their father had insisted. Nina, fifteen and our only daughter, evaded the command by promising to stay home to unpack the dishes and put the kitchen in order.

Most of the heavy items had been loaded when a couple of Bud's friends came by to ask if he could go with them to a softball game. I hated to take up his whole weekend, so I let him go. Tom and I were left to finish up the job.

It wasn't too long before I heard rumblings coming from Tom's direction. He dumped what was left of Stan's tools into a big box and asked angrily, "Why isn't Dad over here helping us?"

I had asked Stan earlier if he would go over to the old house to clean the basement so that I could stay home to unpack boxes. I had to be back at my job on Monday. It would take a lot of time to organize a household for six people, and once my work began again, I would only have the evenings to complete the task. I was already disappointed that I had used up my annual vacation on the move, without finding time to do any relaxing.

Stan had refused to help clean the basement. He said, "You know how much I hate moving and how terrible I'll feel if I go back and see that house again." I understood. Moving made Stan depressed. He had a hard time letting go of things, especially houses. His contribution this day had been to wake the boys early and make them come with me.

All I could say to Tom was, "You know how your

dad hates to move. He was afraid he would get depressed if he came back to the house." Tom became quiet and continued to work. But the cellar was dark, depressing, and dirty—and Tom looked so miserable that I finally said, "I'm mostly finished. Why don't you carry out what's left and drive the truck to the new place? I'll finish up and come over in the car."

It hadn't looked like three hours' work, but it was four o'clock when I pulled into our driveway. No one was home. There was a note on the refrigerator letting me know that Stan, Nina, and Tom had gone bicycling. The dishes hadn't been unpacked.

I rummaged around for a pot to boil some water to make myself a cup of coffee, hoping for one more burst of energy before the day was over. I was angry that they had the leisure to play while I did not. Yet I had been the one who had let them off the hook.

I ignored my anger because I knew that once those people walked back through the door my resentment would disappear. I loved them.

In many ways, we were an unusual family. We did not appear to be much different from other families, especially when the children were small, but as the children matured, more problems arose with each of us than our family circumstances appeared to justify. It was a matter of the unit being more "regular" than its parts. Our children functioned very well within the family structure, but found coping with the outside world difficult.

We were close, caring, and supportive of one another and did many activities together. These qualities caused other young people to try to adopt us as their family. We were tolerant of each other's individual quirks; we allowed and respected differences. It was, perhaps, this tolerance that attracted others to us, and it was this tolerance that ultimately caused our troubles.

I began unpacking cups and saucers and placing them in the cupboard. I knew why I hadn't asked Stan to do more than the loading and unloading of the furniture. I was trying to prevent him from going into a depression over the move. For a good portion of our marriage, he had had spells of depression and anxiety. I did what I could to prevent it or mitigate it. I was doing so now. I was allowing him to "play" to soften his suffering. I was glad, too, that Nina had gone with her father bicycling. It was worth putting the dishes away to give her this opportunity to be with her father. She so often felt ignored by him, especially when he was depressed. She, too, occasionally felt anxiety and mild depression. I was worried about her.

It was my son John, however, who gave me the most concern. He didn't seem to fit well in any context but his home. Most of the time he was a loving, well-behaved, cheerful young man, but at other times his behavior was nothing short of outrageous. I reassured myself by believing that he was a highly intelligent, sensitive, creative person who shouldn't have his uniqueness stifled.

They were special people, these children and this husband of mine. I did what I could to smooth the rough spots in their lives. Why? Because I was an *enabler*! I say this with both distress and embarrassment. It is a crushing admission.

An enabler is one who prevents growth and learning in others by assuming their responsibilities. An enabler promotes weakness in others by protecting them from the consequences of their unproductive behavior.

2

Traits of an Enabler

THE VARIETY OF enabling situations is as infinite as the combinations of relationships—husband-wife, lovers, friends, parent-child, teacher-student, employer-employee, government-constituents, and so on.

However, while enabling is an ageless, genderless pattern of behavior, women perhaps assume the pattern more often than men. Their maternal instincts and their customary function as family caretakers make them naturals for this role. Women are also less likely to believe they can have direct power over their own lives, and encouraging dependency in others can offer them a large measure of control without upsetting traditional roles.

People in a position of responsibility toward others who may require some form of help are in danger of being caught in an enabling trap. The spouse, parent, friend or caretaker of someone who is physically, mentally, or emotionally ill is especially at risk. The line between help which is needed and help which is enabling is often difficult to discern. *The person who supports someone who is capable of standing on his or her own is an enabler.*

Enablers often believe themselves to be victims. But enablers actively choose their dependents and their situations. People don't become enablers by innocently strolling down the pathway of life and being accosted by those who are weak and dependent! They are not coerced into caring for others. The rewards that enablers receive for enabling obviously outweigh the troubles and additional work caused by it or they wouldn't enable. Society extols "do-gooders." Enablers not only show the world their superior altruistic character, but also their competence. Individuals who are capable of assuming the responsibilities of many other people are indeed impressive. As such, they get a collective pat on the back and boost to their self-esteem.

Enabling is a learned way of being. The process of socializing children to become cooperative adults too often fosters "pleasers." As children, we are rewarded for doing what we are told to do and for giving in to the demands of others. Being a pleaser is a very common technique employed by children to cope with childhood pressures. If giving in to the other person consistently brings rewards, this mode of interaction will be continued into adulthood as enabling. The child who is a pleaser has learned to put everyone else first, and responds to the reward of their approval. The child who is not raised in this pattern responds to the more healthy reward of being free to exercise his or her own imagination and desires.

Enablers work at being virtuous and righteous. They exhibit many apparently wonderful qualities. They are adaptable, tolerant, sacrificing, hard-working, kind, tough, courageous, capable, forgiving, and wise. Their multitudinous "virtues" are enough to gag a normally functioning person!

I don't mean to imply that these traits are not valuable

or worthy, but their application does require scrutiny. Each of these virtues has a dark side. One person's exaggerated capabilities can make another person feel incompetent. Forgiveness can breed guilt. Kindness may imply obligation. Tolerance often fosters abuse. Flexibility can take away limits, and strength allows dependency.

Enablers choose the role of the pleaser, sometimes to the point of allowing others to gain pleasure by physically abusing them. The pleaser role may have little to do with any sincere desire to be virtuous. This mode of pleasing is more likely a mechanism for reinforcing attachments.

Our society has taught us to admire the "helping traits" without question. However, if we look at them more critically, we begin to see some of their hidden, less admirable aspects.

Sacrificing

There was an occurrence that happened regularly in the family of my childhood, and I have only recently understood its significance. When we had chicken for dinner, my mother always chose the neck. I thought that this was because she preferred it. While visiting her recently, I served dinner and automatically put the chicken neck on her plate. I was startled to hear her say, with the honesty that comes with age, that she had always *hated* the neck.

Mama's getting the "neck of the chicken" was the common pattern in all of our family interactions. I began to remember that she always *chose* "the neck," the worst part, no matter what goods were being shared or what tasks were being distributed. My mother thought she was being unselfish; actually all that she was being was *last*. Now, I believe that *last* should be an equal opportunity position, shared by all parties.

Tolerant

The children of my friend Jo could win awards if prizes were offered for sloppiness. They walk into the house after fixing the car, throw their greasy shoes on the carpet, sit nonchalantly on the sofa when they are covered with grime, walk into the kitchen and slosh milk into a glass, then drip milk all the way up the stairs and into their bedrooms. Jo patiently follows behind them, trying to undo the damage. Being the family maid doesn't bother her. She gets "rewards" from being tolerant of almost any behavior from almost anyone. She has learned to believe that the shortest route to sainthood is through martyrdom to a noble cause and that the welfare of her family is a noble cause. So she sits at the kitchen table, staring at the mess, and eats another donut and gains another pound.

Being tolerant of inconsiderate people is not sainthood—it is self-punishment.

Adaptable

A group of friends and I have a regular dinner date. Of course, when a group gets together for a meal, the question "Where shall we eat?" arises. Beth always says that it doesn't make very much difference to her where we eat. The rest of us, therefore, take turns picking our favorite spots. Consequently, Beth never gets to go where she wants to eat. By being so "adaptable," she turns over the fun of choosing to everyone else. It is nice of her to do this, but there is no need. There are plenty of times in this world when we can and should compromise, but continually adapting to others' desires is not compromise. This behavior simply fosters a loss of respect for the person who chooses to be the "doormat" and the trait of selfishness in the ones who always get their way.

Hardworking

People who take on the project of a dependent or a family of dependents *have* to be hardworking. They care for the house and children, manage the family's business affairs, tend to the needs and desires of dependents, and are sometimes their only financial support. They do the work of two, maybe three, maybe more.

Norma, who works in a restaurant that I frequently visit, is both a joy and a pain for me to watch. She seems tireless. When it is slow in the restaurant, she takes time to tell me the latest episode of her family saga. Norma works. Her income is never quite enough to meet the family's expenses. Her husband has no interest in finding a job.

Norma cleans the house and takes care of her grandchild when she goes home. Her carefree daughter maintains an active social life. Her son, who has gone off into the world to "find himself," needs a little quick cash telegraphed to him now and then. Norma is constantly juggling the family finances because her small earnings have to support so many people. I ask her (in nicer language), "Why do you support these deadbeats?" She replies, "What can you do?"

Capable

One of my husband's friends, Ray, is a man of many abilities. He is capable of figuring out almost any task from plumbing to home accounting. When he mentions his interactions with his sons about household odd jobs, there are two themes that consistently emerge. One is his grumbling about how he has to do everything for them, and the other is his laughing at the funny mistakes they make in doing simple tasks—always leaving him in the position of having to complete their botched projects.

I have been around Ray when he has been advising his sons about work on their cars. Before, in the middle of, and after the project, Ray gave shrewd advice on how it could be done better, differently, or more completely. He seemed unable to restrain himself from butting into their projects. Any outside observer can see why he ends up doing all of the work around his house! I know his sons well, and Ray's always having one more suggestion has taken a heavy toll on their self-esteem. In the guise of helper, their father has succeeded only in making them feel incompetent.

Courageous and Tough

The enabler employs courage day after day, as she faces not only her own dragons but also the dragons of her husband, children, or friends. Her children don't have to fight their battles on the playground because Mom will talk to the teacher, principal, or other parents, or will threaten the offending children. The enabler's husband doesn't have to face the boss because she will make a special appointment to ask that her husband be given one more chance. The enabler's friend doesn't have to give the report to the PTA, because the enabler has agreed to give it for her.

A classic case of enabling is the wife of an alcoholic who uses her for his punching bag. She is a tough lady.

She has to be, to be bruised over and over again and still go back for more. It takes courage to walk into a fist. It takes courage to go out in the middle of the night in a dangerous neighborhood checking all of the bars for a delinquent husband. It takes courage to lie to his boss the next day, saying that her husband "has a cold."

This courage, which could be her most precious ally, should be used in defending herself, rather than encouraging the vices of others.

Forgiving

An enabler's master virtue is forgiveness. "To err is human and to forgive divine." It is easy to guess who gets which label in this scenario. Such platitudes lend both comfort and perverse, smug pride to the offended enabler. Pretending to forgive—and I say "pretend" because real forgiveness is not what enablers offer— can heap enough guilt on a dependent to cow him for a lifetime.

I thought my mother forgave my father over and over again, because she always allowed him back into her good graces. I believe, now, that only after his death did she truly forgive him.

Wise

A casual glance at any dependency relationship is deceptive. The outward cues lead us to believe that the enabler is the one who is stable and exercising good judgment and common sense. His co-dependent's abilities appear questionable. It is ironic that the one who allows himself to be used like a workhorse can be considered wise. If the enabler has all of the answers, why is it so easy for his dependent to cause him to jump through hoops? Is being a drudge, punching bag, patsy, or doormat wise?

I was recently involved in a business transaction with an elderly gentleman who, during the course of our interaction, voiced his concern about the future of his business. He mentioned that he had always been the only member of the family considered smart enough to keep the business in the black. He had therefore never included anyone else in company decision making. He wanted to retire but couldn't; the rest of the family insisted he continue his position because he had "such good judgment." Meanwhile, his family had plush and carefree lives as the result of encouraging him to believe that only he could run the business competently. He may appear to all the world as having good sense, but it appears to me that his family has outfoxed him.

Loving

It elicits a look of shock to ask an enabler, under any circumstance, why she takes on the role of pleaser, family warrior, facilitator, or caretaker. The answer is so obvious to the enabler that she cannot imagine anyone not seeing it as she does. The question is an insult. The enabler takes care of others out of *love*. She would do anything for those who "need" her. The enabler casts a powerful protective shield of love over her loved ones, unaware that they are being smothered. Even love has its dark side.

Helen, one of the women I work with, has a charming thirty-two-year-old daughter, Jenny, who lives with her. Jenny is Helen's reason for living. It is apparent to anyone enjoying their company how deeply Helen loves her daughter. Helen is constantly taking Jenny on trips, buying her clothes and luxuries, and in general showing her love in every possible way.

Helen is a very happy person. Jenny has a subtle look of desperation in her eyes. She is her mom's beloved toy. Jenny is so in debt to the goodness and giving of her mother that she can never leave her. That Helen can't see and feel Jenny's desperation has made me question the nature of "real love." Helen will give Jenny anything, except her freedom and independence.

Maintaining such a virtuous personality is essential to the enabler's sense of self-worth. But it demands all kinds of sacrifices. Basic, normal interchanges are frustrated. He or she must suppress or ignore personal needs. An enabler's anger has to be swallowed, because he or she is without an honest way to communicate and relate to others on an equal basis. If the enabler is being abused by the dependent, the indignities and hurts compound and continue to fester until they initiate a crisis.

This incredible blending of saintly martyr, weak victim, and superhero is the confusing profile of the enabler. We are playing a game that no one wins!

Portrait of a Dependent

I MET STAN when I was sixteen years old and I knew that one day I would marry him. It wasn't a pressing thing, it was just a conviction I had.

Stan had all of the traits that I wanted in a husband. He was kind, intelligent, full of humor, and had a special quality which I called nobility. Most important, he was not like my father. We had a very strong sense of camaraderie and sharing from the beginning.

He, like me, came from an alcoholic family. His home life had been different from mine in that his mother had not been an emotionally strong woman. Mine was. When his father was drinking, their household fell apart. As a result, Stan suffered the effects of alcoholism more intensely than I did—or so I thought at the time. But, in fact, while he was learning to be anxious and depressed, I was learning to enable.

Stan and I played at romance for about seven years before we finally married. Having both come from homes that were much less than ideal, we did not see marriage as glamorous, so we felt no rush. We did vow, however, that *our* family would never be like those of our childhoods.

An incident that happened before we were married foretold the trouble we would have later, but I was too naive to recognize it. Problems that happen prior to a marriage are often viewed as somehow not real, or as difficulties that will be solved by the marriage (marriage regularly being viewed as a cure-all for a multitude of problems).

We were in our sophomore year at college, attending universities which were fifty miles apart. The separation bothered Stan. He became distraught and came to see me often for comfort and support. In one way, his need was inhibiting, but in another way I loved it. I loved feeling that I was a support for someone, that I was useful, that I was needed.

I spent hours talking him through what had come to be his main concern—what he wanted to do with his life. We discussed this endlessly. What he said he wanted was vague and not specific enough for me. He talked philosophically, while I spoke in practical terms. I was a good listener, and he seemed such a worthy person—I would have done anything to help him.

Stan transferred from his school to mine, and we continued probing his inner feelings in his search for himself. He was nervous and confused, and I felt strong and capable of helping.

Even before we married, I was worried about what our relationship had become, but I was young and thought perhaps we were just going through the normal course of a deepening relationship. I couldn't look to my parents for guidance because they didn't have the kind of marriage I wanted.

There were others I could have married, but besides Stan having all of the qualities I valued, I thought he needed me. I believed that I was the one person who understood him, loved him, appreciated him, and could help him become whatever he chose to become. I knew when I married him that I was taking on a project. But he was so bright and so talented that I expected, with me by his side, that there would be no end to what he could achieve.

I assumed my rewards would come through my husband's accomplishments. Personal fulfillment for a family-oriented woman was having a beautiful house in an affluent neighborhood, a husband who was successful, and children who were on the football team, or winning scholarships. I had been taught this, I believed it, and it felt right. So Stan and I had a common goal—to help him become what he wanted to be. We focused on him. His success would bring family success.

Stan seemed to have been born with a mid-life crisis. He was never sure that he was doing what he was meant to do in life, but as long as he worked hard and kept busy he functioned well and felt good. We were struggling financially. I was having babies at a rapid rate, and Stan was holding down a job and working on an engineering degree. We had created so many responsibilities for ourselves that we could no longer think about which way the stream was going. We just allowed ourselves to be carried along by the current.

As we moved through those early years of struggle, Stan did well. I didn't. Being tied down with four small children was isolating me more and more. I had developed an image of myself as perpetually plump or pregnant. Simply taking my children to the supermarket was overwhelming. Going on a family picnic had become a burden. I was gradually becoming a recluse, beginning to feel unsure of myself in social situations. During this period, Stan never seemed to be home, and I rarely left the house. When he was home, he seemed distracted and ill at ease. He couldn't bear not to be working, and I thought his discomfort (from being at loose ends) meant that he preferred not being with me and the children. I felt that the world was passing me by and taking my husband along.

Our roles had reversed. I had become desperately in need of his attention and time, and he was busy. I had become his burden. The game was the same, but we had switched positions.

Then something with the impact of an emotional earthquake happened, shifting the structure again. Stan completed his doctorate in engineering. It should have brought him relief and rejoicing, but instead, it brought a job decision—which translated into a life decision—and Stan faltered.

Up to this point, Stan had been able to put off making a job decision while working to finish his degree. When he was offered a post on the West Coast that he wanted to take, he was paralyzed. He had been carrying submerged feelings of confusion from being raised in a confused household. These feelings surfaced again.

Stan had spent his childhood with unstable parents moving from one place to another, and he had grown to fear any household move. This opportunity, to which he was so drawn, required moving to an area of the country that was new to us. He now had to make a decision between his present job, which wouldn't require a move, and the new offer, which he wanted. Neither option, however, offered the opportunity to contribute to society in the grandiose manner which he had envisioned, and he began to be sucked back into his "meaning of life" trauma.

Stan spent sleepless nights pacing the floor, talking to me incessantly about the question of moving. He dredged up all of his old fears and worries about his desire to do something significant. It became once more the consuming preoccupation of us both.

Stan became obsessed with his dilemma and was becoming increasingly dysfunctional. He made the decision repeatedly to accept the new appointment. He had to make it "repeatedly," because he was unable to follow through with it.

His friends began avoiding him because his only topic of conversation was his anxiety over trying to make a career decision. He would also seek out people to ask their advice. I shared this obsession and allowed it to become mine.

Because I was preoccupied with Stan, I increasingly ignored the children. All the daily problems and natural happenings in the family became secondary. As his anxiety grew, I took on the task of manipulating our environment so that he would be relieved of any unnecessary emotional distress.

It is said, "trouble never leaves you where it finds you," and while Stan was going through one of the most devastating periods of his life, I was going through a metamorphosis. As friends and acquaintances were changing their opinions of Stan, they were also changing their opinions of me. I was being praised for my strength, courage, calmness, patience, understanding, selflessness, competence, and wisdom. I had become a heroine! And I was needed and loved by my husband! How's that for snatching victory out of the jaws of defeat?

We moved to the West Coast and sought medical help for Stan's anxiety. We learned that his prolonged unresolved situation had triggered a chemical depression. Gradually, he recovered his equilibrium and our life began to normalize, but the trauma had altered us both. He was demoralized and insecure about his abilities, and lived continuously on the verge of depression. I, although living in fear that I couldn't forever keep juggling the needs and demands of Stan, the children, and the wolf at the door, was gathering strength.

A shift in the family dynamic had occurred. Life had returned to the way it had been in the early part of our marriage. I was in control, and it was an easy role for me, a natural role, the role that my mother had filled.

The years that followed continued to be somewhat troubled. Stan was in and out of depression, and I was again in the position of trying to make a sad man happy.

I worked hard at trying to pull Stan out of his depression, but everything I did seemed to produce an effect opposite to what I had intended. The more cheerful I acted, the more morose he became. When I offered a positive solution, he would tell me that the only reason I could have made such a foolish suggestion was because I didn't fully understand the situation.

Stan didn't want to be consoled; he wanted me to participate in his sadness. He needed me not only to keep his physical environment intact but to support his emotional drama. Stan was clearly a *dependent*.

A dependent is one who is unwilling to accept responsibility for his or her own situation. A dependent expects others to provide for his or her well-being.

4

Traits of a Dependent

WHILE EACH DEPENDENCY situation has its own peculiarities, dependents share many attributes. Dependents' individual responses to any particular situation might vary in detail, but their overall patterns of behavior are similar. Therefore, dependent people have their own distinguishing characteristics, just as enablers do.

Because dependency can have both constructive and destructive parameters, it is important before we go further in this discussion to draw a distinction between healthy interdependence and parasitic dependency.

Interdependence is a natural state that every human being experiences, in various degrees, throughout his or her life. All children require the support of adults. During illness, we all expect others to care for us or release us from our work commitments. Many in old age must rely on the support and care of others. We all know what it feels like to be interdependent. We know this not only because of these common life situations, but also because our society's survival rests on interdependence. We urban folk would all starve if the transportation system bringing our food from the farms were destroyed. Social interdependence is a necessary and positive factor of our lives.

Interdependence in the family and working community is also necessary and desirable. The hard-working mother who manages a home and family is a fully participating, contributing member of that unit. Her working husband, who might be the only wage-earner in the household, is nevertheless as dependent on her contribution as she is on his. They share the responsibilities for the survival of their family. Their children depend on them for love and support, material well-being, and moral guidance. They also depend on their children to love and support them and each other, to act responsibly at school and home, and to share domestic duties.

These natural, necessary interdependencies which ensure our survival are not what I mean when I refer to the type of dependence which is the other half of an enabling co-dependence.

The term *co-dependent* is used by counselors to define people who need and use others to maintain nonproductive and self-defeating behaviors. It is a parasitic relationship—the *dependent* needing (or wanting) someone to take over his or her responsibility to society, and the *enabler* needing (or wanting) to take over another's responsibility in order to bolster his or her own sagging self-image. *Just as an enabler needs to have a problem to solve, a dependent needs to have a problem.*

Why anyone would *need* to have problems is a curious issue and quite complicated. For our purpose, we only need to know that there are many people whose lives revolve around "unsolvable" problems. When one such person turns his or her problems over to another to handle—in essence saying, "take care of me"—a cycle of dependence begins.

Dependent persons need to have a "reason" for being parasitically dependent, which they can use to justify their behavior not only to society but also to themselves. Being parasitically dependent includes much more than economic dependence. Emotional parasitism is perhaps more deadly to families and individuals than economic dependence. People who have retreated from interaction with the world and live off the emotional and spiritual experiences of others suck the very life and energy from them.

While the reasons used for being dependent vary widely, they generally tend to cluster in categories such as: illness and disability, grief over tragedy or failure, negative factors from outside ("the world is against me"), laziness, or an "I'm special" attitude.

People who are chronically ill or are disabled appear to have a straightforward, airtight reason for dependence. Yet their claims may be justified or not. We believe, as a society, that all people have an obligation to contribute what they can and to be responsible within the range of their abilities for their own physical and emotional lives. Our society feels responsible for the care of the sick and disabled, but makes heroes of people who overcome handicaps on their own. Those who allow themselves to use their illness or disability as an excuse to shirk their responsibilities to do *what they can* for themselves fit our definition of dependent.

Grief over tragic events or devastating failures is acceptable to society as a reason to be temporarily dependent. After an appropriate length of time, however, those who grieve are expected to face the present and move on with their personal and professional lives.

People who claim that they could go out into the world and slay dragons, if it weren't for everything and everybody conspiring against them, place the blame for their dependence on forces outside themselves. They pretend the world *won't let them* succeed. Why should they try?

The person who refuses to work unless he is offered the job of corporation president believes he is a special person. The person who feels that she should be allowed to bully her family or friends with impunity believes that the rules are for others. Special people feel that the world owes them special consideration. The special and lazy usually don't find it necessary to offer reasons for being dependent on others. It is obvious to them that they deserve endless tolerance and support.

Whatever the reason given by a dependent for his or her situation, something has to be cited as being wrong. Perpetually having something wrong, whether it is real or imagined, reinforces the dependent's negative attitude. Having to continually justify their dependence, both internally and to others, pushes the dependent deeper and deeper into discontent.

People do suffer illness, have accidents, lose loved ones, are born with handicaps, and simply suffer failures and misfortune. These are the realities of the human condition. We all must accept that one or all of these catastrophes will happen to us or to someone we love at one time or another.

It is the difference in response to life's catastrophes that separates the dependent from the individual who accepts loss, readjusts, and begins again to contribute according to his or her ability. Parasitic dependents will grasp the trauma as an excuse for inaction and withdrawal from the responsibility of contributing their fair share. Using past tragedies or failures to avoid dealing with the present is a frequent technique of neurotically dependent people. They always have some past battle to fight. As in shadow boxing, their struggling jabs don't connect with anything real or solid.

At the root of dependence is the dependent's insecurity about his or her abilities. Dependents may show a great deal of energy in thrashing about for a solution to the particular problems that have made them dependent, but the bottom line is that they are afraid they can't make it without help. Therefore, there is no real drive toward a solution or change. Should others offer solutions and possibilities to a confirmed dependent, these suggestions will be met with every objection conceivable. All dependents have their reasons for *working at, but not finding,* a solution to their dependence, and they all boil down to fear: fear of change, fear of failure, fear of losing the enabler, fear of independence.

Dependents, by being unwilling to face the world on the world's terms, abdicate that responsibility to someone else, thus placing themselves under the control of others.

Dependents who feel depressed and defeated often accuse others of taking a "Pollyanna" approach to life, of being simple-minded. When someone swings into the "looking at the positive side" mode, he or she is often treated like a fool for being naïve. It took me a number of years to come to the realization that being a Pollyanna was not only acceptable, but a preferable way to react to life's upsets. Needing to have something wrong in order to justify one's behavior is inherently a negative attitude. If, as Idealist philosophers assert, life *is* what one perceives it to be, why not perceive it to be bountiful and benevolent? An optimistic attitude can help produce happiness. If what you see is what you get, it makes eminently more sense to see good than bad. At a practical level, this philosophy *is* very "simple." Those who see living as a pleasant experience are able to have more pleasant lives. Those who insist on viewing living as painful and difficult will find pain and difficulty in whatever circumstances they encounter.

I spent hours with Stan trying to help him work out a plan of action which would allow him to step out of his circular obsession and move forward. I was looking for results; he was avoiding results.

Stan felt victimized by an unfair world that would not offer him the exact job he wanted in the precise location he chose. To him, there was no solution to this problem, and although he finally had to compromise, in his heart there was no compromise. I erroneously believed during this time of decision trauma that Stan wanted to make a decision and that he wanted me to help. In hindsight, I see that all of his flailing about was done to protect him from having to make a decision. What he wanted from me was not help to find a practical solution but someone to participate in his grief.

A dependent cannot remain a dependent if he or she has no one to depend upon. In order to maintain any degree of dependence, a dependent needs the support of an enabler.

Nancy, Stan's secretary, has a twenty-four-year-old son, Tim, who manages to land in jail at least once a year. He is never thrown in jail (according to Nancy) for anything major, just piddling infractions of the law. Nancy becomes very irritated with the police because she believes that they have something against her son. Over and over again, she bails Tim out. When Stan comes home and tells me of Tim's latest brush with the law, I find myself becoming angry with Nancy rather than Tim. She constantly prevents him from learning the lessons he needs to learn if he wants to stay out of jail. Every friend, employer, counselor, and casual acquaintance has advised Nancy to leave him in jail to pay for his offense. She simply can't bring herself to do it.

When people like Tim are not required to alter their

unproductive behavior because they are protected from its natural consequences, it is easy for them to become dependent. Their experience of the world is that the world will always accommodate them.

The alcoholic is the classic example of the dependent who needs the support of others to maintain dependent life patterns. Alcoholics, who find a mate who will accommodate their behavior, can spend a lifetime without changing. They have someone strong and capable they can depend upon to hold things together, cover for them, and protect them from the consequences of alcoholism. Dependents believe themselves to be victims of an uncaring world, when actually they are victims of an overprotective one.

We all learn very early in life which behaviors get us the strokes we need. If we are unable to get the strokes we want, we settle for those we can get, and we use whatever tactic it takes to get them. As we move through adulthood, we carry our early childhood pattern of behavior with us, reforming it as we go according to the rewards and punishments we receive from society. While many of us will jump fearlessly into the adult world, dependents are reluctant and will check first to see if they really want to participate. If the adult world appears too frightening, they will develop a nonparticipating strategy for protection.

Stan confided that when his father was drinking, he became so engrossed in his own drama that he ignored Stan. When Stan exhibited sadness or anxiety over his father's drinking, he would be noticed. Because Stan's childhood needs were not being met in the course of daily living, his only way of getting attention was to be more distraught than his parents were. He has said that he often felt lost as a child.

A child from a home where catastrophe is a regular part of life can easily carry for the rest of his or her life the fear that catastrophe is around every corner. Others seem to be leading happy, normal lives, but the troubled children feel like victims who have been cheated out of some essential emotional element which is required for enjoyable living. They don't know why their lives are different, and they have a deep-seated feeling that they have done something wrong or that they are unworthy. They feel that they are not understood. It is easy to see how, under such circumstances, a person can grow up believing that life is a continuing trauma and that the only way to be acknowledged is to be depressed or unhappy.

Struggling for independence in a competitive world is difficult for everyone. Children who have never been allowed to make their own mistakes and rectify them are as ill prepared for life as children with an inadequate parental model. They will continue into adulthood looking for protectors who will allow them to make the same mistakes.

Dependents are afraid to change because they are insecure about their own abilities. They feel miserable and become stuck in those feelings without moving on. Their pain seems so genuine and their situation so unbearable that others are easily pulled into their trauma. Enablers will stick with them and help them perpetuate that trauma. Other friends listen, offer suggestions, and do what they can to help—until they realize that what the dependent seeks is not a solution, but the attention that misfortune brings. At that point, the friends move on and away, and the dependent must look for new friends.

Insecure dependents use their needs to keep others tied to them, making it hard for giving, feeling people to abandon them. It is very difficult for an enabler to break this spell. On some level dependents know this, and they are able to keep their spouses, parents, children, or friends tied to them indefinitely. A sick man who feels that his wife will leave him may move from one illness to another to keep her, consciously unaware of what he is doing. He only knows that he feels ill and can't survive without her, and he makes sure that she knows that he desperately needs her.

While we enablers are rather drab characters, being practical rule-followers and hard workers, our dependents are often romantic figures, perpetually preoccupied with their own dramas. To me, my husband was a magnificent, stricken eagle—and I very often felt like a domestic duck. Being reliable and predictable can be a bore to others. Stan often said, "I hate the word 'adjust.' It is like someone going into my head with a wrench and tightening screws or loosening bolts. Why should I adjust?" I never had an answer. Somehow, his indignation over this seemed justified. The world should have been more accommodating. *I* was.

His question not only kept me in my place, it also haunted me. It was in one of those "ah-ha" flashes that the answer came to me: One doesn't have to adjust! But there is a heavy price to be paid for not doing so. Stan was paying the price and borrowing the "money" from me.

We each have the right to behave as we wish, but all types of behavior have consequences. There are natural laws governing mutually rewarding interaction with others, and there are social customs that have developed for the good of the whole. These principles, with their system of rewards and punishments, form the ecology of our emotional world. We can accept or reject established patterns, but we don't have the option of rejecting the consequences; the consequences always follow!

If one is not willing to accept the results of a particular type of behavior, he or she must change the behavior. The consequence of not adjusting to the reality of one's world is that one is prevented from fully participating in it. Dependent people are "nonplayers." Enablers play their parts for them.

Nonparticipating people who have become dependent because they are ill or disabled should be encouraged to do and produce as much as they are able. Those who are depressed or exhibit erratic behavior could be suffering from a chemical or organic disorder which needs medical attention. These people are not battling "strength of character" issues, but disease. They need help in learning how to monitor their emotions and seek medical aid when they feel they are losing control.

However, those who are dependent from fear and poor self-esteem need counseling and support groups. Those who are lazy or too "special" to work may need to miss a few meals. The one thing none of them needs is an enabler who supports their dependence and prevents them from learning how to handle their own lives.

5

My Son John

I HAD LIVED through an earthquake—Stan's depressive breakdown—and was still standing, just tall enough to be struck by lightning. Being struck by lightning is the most apt analogy I can find to express how a family feels when one of its members has a mental breakdown.

It began in the summer before John's twentieth birthday. He suddenly became very ill and felt highly agitated. He believed that one of his friends had slipped a drug, perhaps angel dust, into something he was drinking.

John became so frightened and paranoid that he was unable to sleep at night in his own bedroom. Instead he would go into the bathroom, which had no windows, lock the door, and sleep on the floor. He felt so vulnerable when asleep that he was soon almost never sleeping. His growing fatigue began making it hard for him to go to his summer job, and when he went, it was difficult for him to remain the entire day. As his conviction that he had been poisoned grew into an obsession, he started working out with weights to increase his strength in case he needed to protect himself.

Watching him pace back and forth in the living room almost at a run, I became confused and afraid. I didn't know what to believe or how to react to what he was doing. It was not beyond the realm of possibility that there had been a very cruel trick played on him, triggering a chemical imbalance in his brain. Whatever precipitated John's frenzied disorientation, it was the most severe tragedy I could have imagined.

We had taken John to a physician two months previously for a severe disabling headache. He was hospitalized for a day, given medication for pain, and told that he had a cluster headache which would eventually go away. It did. When he first became agitated and claimed that he had been poisoned, we took him to a psychiatrist. Having dealt with drug-related psychosis, the doctor believed there might well be a possibility that John's distress and paranoia were the result of a toxic substance. A blood test didn't indicate there was anything unusual in his system, however, so there was nothing we could do but wait and observe his behavior.

Then John called us one day from a pay phone near his job and said, "Come to get me, I've been wandering around." We called his psychiatrist, who made arrangements for him to be admitted to a hospital. When we picked him up, we didn't bring him home. We drove one hundred miles to the nearest psychiatric hospital which had an opening.

After leaving him in the hospital, I was enveloped by that heavy blackness that descends on those who have lost, to death, the most precious person in their lives. But grieving over death is cleaner and clearer. Tragic disabling illness produces sorrow mixed with terror and panic. Stan was quiet and tried to comfort me. But he, too, was heartbroken and beaten. I was good at handling crises, but this was far beyond me. I found it unbelievable that my handsome young boy, with so much promise, could be stricken so disastrously and swiftly.

John was our middle son. He had always been very creative and bright. His early childhood had been filled with active, happy play. After we moved into a country home, his main interest had been raising animals for Four-H projects, and through that experience he had developed a sensitive, accepting, and warm nature.

He seemed so responsive and loving that I didn't allow myself to see any out-of-the-ordinary traits he may have had. I missed the telltale signs that should have warned me of trouble ahead for him. If I did notice anything unusual in his behavior, I always passed it off as unimportant.

As Johnny was growing up, my interaction with him was similar to my interaction with my husband. I allowed him his weaknesses, covered for him, did his household chores, and anticipated his needs. I had rationalized his dropping out of school during his senior year and welcomed him home without question when he failed to complete basic training in the army.

While *I* had been willing to overlook John's occasionally aberrant behavior, others had not. He had an insatiable craving for attention. When Stan was feeling well he spent many hours with John, helping with various animal projects. When Stan was in one of his depressions, however, it was difficult for anyone to reach him. He ignored his surroundings, including his children. The other children responded by staying out of his way and going about their business, but it was always important to John to have contact with his father. He would follow Stan around and talk incessantly, trying to get a response. Sometimes this was annoying to Stan, but most of the time he wasn't aware that John was even there.

Johnny's need for attention spilled over into his school and social life. His hyperactivity and clownish behavior in the third grade prompted the teacher to suggest that he be medicated with Ritalin to calm him. I became angry and felt that the teacher only wanted him drugged so she wouldn't have to deal with his creativity. Had I not been an enabling mother, I might have been able to recognize that he suffered from a pathological hyperactivity. I might have sought help for him earlier. His outbursts of outlandish behavior continued until, as a teenager, he would do or say outrageous things merely for shock value.

I chided him when he did something absurd, and the word chide is so right for what I did. My chiding was an ineffectual admonition that implied that his behavior could be continued without any serious consequence.

It wasn't until the summer after John came home from the hospital that an incident occurred which forced me to look at myself and see some of my responsibility for his unacceptable behavior.

A group of family and friends was gathered in our living room. John began making outrageous comments designed to embarrass his sister and me. When I mentioned the incident later to my youngest son, Bud, he told me in a burst of anger that it was my fault that John didn't know how to behave. He said I had allowed him his excesses. I had ignored them, pretended I didn't hear, called them a phase, but I had never said, "Stop!"

I decided to see if Bud was right. I talked to John and told him that his comments during that incident had been completely unacceptable to me and that I would not allow him to speak that way in my house again. John was stunned and quiet, and that sort of incident did not happen again. In spite of his illness, he understood and accepted limits.

During those years in which I thought I was such a kind, tolerant, loving mother, I had enabled him to develop a pattern of behavior that was unacceptable to others outside his family. John had so many endearing qualities that it had been too easy for me to overlook and forgive his unusual behavior. He was loved and had been tolerated by the whole family.

John was diagnosed as bipolar manic. I can see now that the seed of the illness was always within him and that the illness is the result of factors far beyond my control. While I didn't cause the illness, I did promote it, in the same way that I fed my husband's depression. I had tried to protect them from the demands of their environment; what they needed was to learn to face their problems and accommodate their illnesses to the realities and demands of the world.

I lived through Stan's and John's traumas—I made them my own. There were many times during the years of juggling the whole mess that I thanked God that I had been there for them and had been strong enough to handle the burden. I didn't know that God would have been likely to reply: "Would you get the hell out of the way, so I can help these people learn to help themselves?"

6

The Turning Point

DURING THOSE DARK days, I scurried around trying to do what I could to maintain the stability of my family. I didn't know what to do to help Johnny, and I didn't know how to handle the new circumstances which now dramatically affected each one of us. The situation was too serious to allow myself to blunder through it, and I no longer trusted my own judgment.

My personal search intensified. I reviewed every self-help program available to me. While I felt that they all offered me some new bit of understanding, it was an interplay of seemingly unrelated family events that brought me the insight I needed to change my way of relating to others.

My son's illness had done several things to me. Most important, it put everything else into perspective. All other problems seemed like minor irritations by comparison. Even my husband's bouts with depression seemed inconsequential. In the past, helping Stan through one of those periods had been the principal struggle of my life. I now found myself catapulted into a different state of mind. Only Johnny's pain (he was going through so much of it) and my own grief were important to me.

Family life, although irrevocably altered, was settling down. I began again to do the routine things that make up the day-to-day existence of middle-class living. Yard work and house repair which had been postponed now needed my attention. I called a tree specialist to spray our trees for bark beetles. After looking at the trees, the tree surgeon suggested we cut down a particularly large pine in the front yard that was still quite beautiful but badly infested. I knew we needed firewood, so without much thought I had Bud and one of his friends cut it down for me.

When Stan came home from work and saw the felled tree, he completely came apart. He was very angry with me. He hadn't wanted the tree cut. Despite the tree surgeon's advice, Stan thought he could have saved it. He began doing what, in the past, had brought me to my knees and to his side—he went into a depression over the loss of the tree. He walked around randomly in a completely distraught state and refused to be comforted. It was a pattern of behavior I had become familiar with and accustomed to since our college days. I had seen him through dozens of such periods.

There was something different this time, however, and the difference was me. I was grieving for my son. Johnny was all I could think about, and I didn't give a damn about that tree. I looked at Stan, and for the first time, instead of looking pathetic to me, he looked foolish. Then I became angry. How dare he mount this big production over a tree when his son was sick in the hospital a hundred miles away. My anger not only kept me from responding sympathetically, but also caused me to lash out at him. I said two things that hit their mark. One was that he was behaving like a spoiled child who hadn't gotten his way. The other was that, while he fancied himself a misunderstood tragic hero, when he was acting like this he appeared to others as simply a nut!

My assertions and my altered attitude, coming on the heels of his own soul-searching about Johnny's condition, produced nothing short of a miracle in Stan. He changed his behavior immediately. I knew that what I had said had been unforgivably cruel, but for the first time in all the years of trying to help him, I actually had.

The tremendous importance of what had just happened didn't sink in immediately because I was still feeling traumatized by what seemed like the loss of my son.

Within the month, a new crisis came into Stan's life. We sold our house. Stan had agreed to sell it earlier because we were a shrinking family in a five bedroom home. We had enjoyed the house for more than four years, but we now needed the money for our children's college expenses.

Stan went into his "moving" trauma again. In the past, I had always agreed to anything to accommodate his feelings. If he said, "I don't want to move," I would reply, "You don't have to; we will figure out some way to do whatever you want to do." This time, when he started into the first phase of what I now call unacceptable behavior, I countered it. I told him, "There is no way you're going to get out of this agreement. We need the money and we don't need the house. I will not back out, and I won't allow you to. If you suffer an anxiety attack, I will put you in the hospital and continue the sale, so you may as well shape up and not sabotage the deal."

As a result of my new attitude, Stan worked to help with the sale of the house—and was later pleased with himself for having done so.

I had begun changing the way I responded to everyone in the family. I put up with less and demanded more. An awareness of how I was changing didn't dawn on me until an interchange took place that involved John and my mother. My mother (eighty-five at the time) was a fragile but very alert woman. She was spending the month with us, as she does annually. That year it wasn't particularly convenient because Johnny was home from the hospital and his behavior wasn't always predictable.

One day Johnny started one of his bizarre episodes and began saying outrageous things to my mother. I became furious with him. That universal instinct, which demands respect for mothers above all other creatures, came over me and I took John aside, sick as he was, and said, "That is my mother. Don't you ever, ever, ever say a negative thing to her, look at her in a strange way, or even think a bad thought about her." I had always listened to his paranoid ramblings about other people, trying to be reasonable and talk him out of his delusions. But this one I would not tolerate, and he knew it. During the rest of my mother's visit he was very respectful.

I was again astonished by the revelation that I didn't *have* to allow John to do as he pleased just because he was ill. This may be a simple observation to most people, but to a consummate enabler it is a powerful insight.

In this instance, my primary concern was my mother. Johnny was secondary. I did what felt instinctively right to me, without trying to justify Johnny's behavior or accommodate his illness. Just as my concern for Johnny had interfered with my giving Stan special attention for his inappropriate behavior, my feelings for my mother had taken priority over John's illness. Both times I forgot my enabling behavior and did what I felt was *just*, letting whatever else might happen as a result, happen.

Instead of trying to manipulate Stan into being happy and John into being respectful, I had let them know that their behavior was unacceptable to me. The process of returning the burden of their behavior back to them had begun.

What I had experienced changed forever the way I saw myself in relation to my family. This fundamental shift in viewpoint precipitated a remarkable change in the way I reacted. I no longer felt compelled to be Stan's and John's keeper. By allowing them to take care of their own needs, I was released from an overwhelming job. It was the best gift I could give to the three of us.

Assessing Myself

THINGS HAPPEN TO you, but you also happen to them. The knowledge that I had allowed, perhaps encouraged, both my son's and my husband's behavior struck me with such force that this truth seemed irrefutable. The scrutiny that I had given them I now had to turn on myself. They had happened to me, but I had also happened to them. I had learned all that I could about their illnesses. It never occurred to me that I might be fostering those illnesses or that my role in the family dynamics represented a sickness too. The concept of personal responsibility is an aspect of every psychological and quasi-psychological theory. Unfortunately, I had focused on the "be responsible for yourself" part and had missed its corollary—"and let others be responsible for themselves."

Why had this obvious understanding of human interaction eluded me? Had I imprinted on a particular role model so early in my life that I was incapable of seeing other models? Did my self-esteem hinge on being responsible for others? It was at this time that a family counselor gave me a book by Janet Geringer Woititz which he thought would be helpful. At first I was put off by the title, *Marriage on the Rocks*, because "on the rocks" referred to alcohol and neither my husband nor I drank. And I didn't like the implication that my marriage was in trouble.

I suppose things come to us when we are ready for them, because that book reached me in a way that nothing else had. The description of the wife of an alcoholic was me. It was incredible to me that Stan and I, who both hated alcohol and swore we would never have a home like the ones we had come from, were portrayed in the pages of this book. We had the same neurotic patterns, without the chemical substance!

An alcoholic is a person with compulsions and a chemical problem. The spouse of an alcoholic, unless he or she has learned to be different, is an enabler. I am an enabler, even though my husband doesn't use alcohol or drugs. Enabling is every bit as much a malady as alcoholism, depression, or mania.

I wasn't born an enabler. Like most people, I learned it by growing up in an environment where it was to my advantage to please. Pleasing others allowed me to manipulate my circumstances to get at least some of what I needed or wanted.

Like many children raised in an alcoholic family, I responded to the situation by being a very helpful, obedient child. I believed that poor behavior on my part would only be an additional burden on our already stressed family. My father's drinking always unsettled me, but mostly I felt sorry for him and sorry for my mother.

I bounced through life believing that I was learning what life was all about from my parents. I watched how they responded to each other and how they raised children. There were things I didn't like about the way my parents conducted their household, and I promised myself that I would never act the way they did or create a home similar to theirs. But I had absorbed their model, unaware that much of my mother's behavior would become my own.

Living on a farm the first few years of my life helped me through the times when things were chaotic in the house—meaning Daddy was drunk—because I had places to go to avoid being under foot. There was plenty to do. I watched at a distance, always telling myself that I would never marry a man like my dad. I worried about my mom, but I knew that she was tough. She was quiet, stoic, and tough.

It was difficult not to follow the pattern my parents had set for me. As an adult, I was often jolted by glimpses of myself mimicking them. I had unwittingly and unwillingly picked up many of their traits.

Examining my childhood now, it is not too difficult to see how I became an enabler. My mother was a self-contained, reliable woman. She was not an affectionate person like my father, but she was consistent and stable. There were times when I knew we were in deep financial trouble and my mother tried to protect us children from knowledge of it. She even protected my father. My father had the luxury of being able to go on his periodic binges because my mother would keep things intact for him. She lived during a difficult era with the huge responsibility of six children. I'm sure she felt that she could not run the risk of rebellion against my father. She didn't know what disasters might follow if she failed to maintain the household when my father faltered. What she did was for her own survival and for the protection of her children.

Accommodating my father's irresponsible behavior

was a big part of the burden my mother carried. I learned how to be a mother and a wife from her. But my life and circumstances are different from hers. Emulating her stoic patterns in my circumstances has not only been ineffective for me, it has been disastrous for my family.

Society also nudged me into the role of enabler. Thousands of subtle cues told me from the time I was born that my principal role as a woman was to serve. It was easy to accept it as the right course and even to become self-righteous about it.

It takes more than pressure from external sources, however, to make us behave consistently in a specific way. Behavior has to fill a need. In spite of the image of strength, competence, and control that I often projected, I was deeply insecure. That insecurity fostered the role I played. I needed to be needed. My self-esteem depended on it. While it is a rare person who doesn't have problems with negative self-esteem at some time, an enabler's lack of self-esteem is much greater than is apparent. Unconsciously, and sometimes consciously, I manipulated the circumstances of my life to place myself in a position of being needed.

People build self-esteem by trying to excel in various ways. If this doesn't work, they will settle for simply being better than the next guy. It is this "better than the next guy" attitude that causes trouble. Too often, getting ahead means pushing someone else behind. *One can't be needed unless there is someone in need.*

People whose self-worth is based on being needed usually begin relationships by choosing as partners or friends those who are dependent and have problems. Such relationships, though often full of torment, can develop a secure and complementary form of stability.

Should the helpers (enablers) actually succeed in helping their dependents, which supposedly was their original goal, their relationships may be weakened, causing them to feel threatened and their partners to become confused. To maintain the bond, enablers may unwittingly sabotage their partners' progress by continuing to treat them as fragile and incompetent and by focusing on their helplessness.

There is a hidden acknowledgment in the enabler's destructive support: A weak partner is better than no partner at all. Thus "strong" partners (enablers) of "weak" dependents may fear that their dependents will indeed become successful and discover they no longer need or want their enablers. Enablers suspect they are only wanted because they are needed. So, unconsciously, they hold on to their dependents (partners, friends, or children) by perpetuating their weaknesses.

I had married Stan, a wonderful young man who needed me. But when he became involved in life and began trading problems for successes, my own sense of worth plummeted. I needed to be an enabler to feel worthy of Stan's respect, but he no longer needed an enabler. He was capably working full time to support me and the children. He was completing his doctorate in engineering. He was associated with a musical group that required his time and talent. Stan needed me—the *real* me—but I had no model for that kind of healthy and equal relationship. So, I became jealous and fearful that I could lose him. I then turned to my children for opportunities to be needed. They got a double dose of overprotection because I had lost my first dependent.

Later, when Stan was struck again with depression, I had him back. When he was under stress, he made me feel like the most valuable person in the world. Even with the fear and panic that his depression brought, I felt the tie was once again secure.

Viewing myself accurately, within the family of my childhood and the family I had created, was an important step for me in appraising my attitudes and reactions. I needed to look at myself without my disguise of the "noble, perfect helper" in order to break the stranglehold of my enabling behaviors.

8

Allowing Others to be Responsible

CONSIDERING THE GREAT number of us who make a muddle of our lives, it would appear that it is simple to make life difficult—and difficult to make life simple. People can become tangled in life's complexities, and it is no surprise that the more one struggles, the more likely one is to get lost in the jumble.

The lucky ones among us are those who feel essentially loved, respected, and worthy because the majority of their experience with others has been supportive and caring. They are free to use their time, energy, and intelligence to work, accomplish, and create—all things that bring satisfaction. Their relationships are open and less complicated, because they can love and be loved freely, without the accompanying games.

It is unfortunate that we all can't have the best possible characteristics and circumstances for a spontaneously happy life. Nonetheless, we must *accept who we are*, and what we have. We may have wished for different parents, or to have been shorter or taller or smarter, but we are what we are. We simply can't choose the size of our feet or the neighborhood to which our parents move. Our only possibilities for change and control grow out of the way we react to what we are given.

Most of us who were not blessed with an optimal combination of innate characteristics and a supportive home life come to terms with our less-than-perfect circumstances and accept ourselves as we are. We adjust very early to our situation and do what works best. Enablers, however, protect or prevent those dependent upon them from having to come to terms with the realities of their lives. They prevent them from taking the essential steps we must all take to become responsible, productive adults.

Stan suffers periodic attacks of endogenous chemical depression. This form of depression has been identified recently as a fairly common disease in contemporary society. Having this propensity to depression is a factor in Stan's life that needs to be understood, accepted, and considered, but not used by him as an excuse. He, like everyone else, needed to accept the unique characteristics with which he was born, acknowledge them, and then make the appropriate adjustments in order to fully participate in living.

Enablers' exaggerated acceptance of their family's or friends' weaknesses simply rewards and encourages the weaknesses. For example, a child who loses the use of his legs should be taught to use a wheelchair, and not to be waited upon. His inability should not be used as an excuse to prevent him from developing all of his possibilities. He is capable of doing many of the activities we all do. An alcoholic may have one limitation only, that she can't drink. A person who is depressed may have little control over feeling despair, but does have the choice of whether to remain in bed or not.

An enabler does everything for the child who can't walk, covers up for the alcoholic, and gives maid service to the person who refuses to get out of bed.

It is difficult for someone with a handicap to want to overcome it if he or she is surrounded by others who are willing to reward it. The enabler becomes one more obstacle, perhaps the biggest obstacle, for the dependent to overcome. A dependent person attached to someone who feeds his or her dependency is doubly disadvantaged.

Stan had to bring his lot in life into agreement with the reality of the world. It was a long, hard struggle, made longer and harder by me. John had to meet the demands of society, notwithstanding his handicap, and he is doing it. But he is having to unlearn some of the behavior I allowed.

John is doing well now. He is finding out about himself. When we were talking recently about his recovery program, he said, "You know, Mom, I'm learning some terrific things." At that moment, he seemed more confident, secure, and happy than I had seen him in a long time. It was sad to think that I could have been of some *real* help to him, had I known and been able to change *my* behavior when he was a child.

John is a bright and capable person who is now working to conquer a difficulty with which he was born. The struggle with hyperactivity that he had as a child was sending him a message about himself. I protected him from receiving it.

For someone like me—whose self-worth was dependent on caring for others—to find that I had actually damaged the people I most loved was a devastating revelation.

Often, in the past, I had wanted to get inside the skins of my children to help them. I felt I was so much more capable of handling their lives than they were.

That I was actually denying them their identity never occurred to me. A sense of identity comes with discovering who we are, and self-esteem comes from developing what we have. I had been usurping their identity and chipping away at their self-esteem in my desire to help them.

On one occasion, I was participating in a counseling session with Stan and Nina. Nina was going through a particularly difficult time, and I had commented on how sorry I was that I hadn't been able to help her be happier. The counselor turned to me and asked, "Are you responsible for your daughter's happiness?" I sputtered a little, without answering. He then turned to Nina and said, "Do you feel it is your mother's responsibility to keep you happy?" Nina said, "No, of course not."

I was surprised that no one but me felt it was my job to keep her happy. Perhaps this attitude was a carry-over from my childhood when I felt the obligation to cheer up my father and mother. If someone wasn't happy, I felt responsible.

It wasn't just the happiness factor I felt responsible for, either. It was everything about their lives. When they hollered "help," I jumped to the rescue and snatched the problem from their hands.

It took many incidents to make it clear to me that I regularly assumed my children's power and stripped them of the challenge of solving their own problems.

I remember one typical episode quite well. I visited Nina at college in Boston. I had always thought of her as a very smart but disorganized girl. Nina seemed to have very little common sense. When she was growing up, I always took care of the practical aspects of her life. I believed I was good at dealing with her daily responsibilities, while she wasn't. When she left for Boston, I was extremely fearful for her, mainly because I wasn't certain she would be able to take care of the logistics of daily survival, like how to catch the correct bus, where to find a place to live, or how to make money transactions. When I visited her, I was surprised to find that she was doing extremely well. In addition to doing well in her classes, she had an apartment and a part-time job.

While I was there, we decided to take the train to New York City. At the station, I was keeping an eye on our luggage while she went to check out schedules. I watched her as she looked at the billboard, puzzled, and I went over to read it for her. I then asked her how she managed when she first came to the city. She replied, "When you are not around Mom, I figure it out, but when you are with me, you seem to do things so much more efficiently, I let you do it." Nina admitted that she always felt incompetent when she was with me because I seemed to be able to do things better than she. That hurt! I, like every parent, wanted my children to grow up feeling confident and good about themselves.

I had spent years trying to protect my daughter from the hurts of the outside world. The one person she wasn't protected from was me.

Stan had always been aware of my enabling behavior toward the children. He felt that I was too lenient and did too much for them. If he ever said anything critical about one of them, I would come to their defense. Of course, if the children berated their father, I also came to his defense. I protected them from each other. Stan worried about our children not having as many responsibilities as he felt they should, but when he would try to talk to me about it, I would behave as if he were attacking me and he wouldn't pursue it. He believed me to be a well-meaning, caring mother and he let it go at that. He never transferred his awareness of my being an enabling mother to a recognition that I was also an enabling wife.

I was good at assigning household tasks to my children, but I was never good at following through. If one of them said, "I'll do it later," when the "later" never came, I would do the chore. If an assignment became inconvenient, difficult, or interfered with their other plans, I rescinded the assignment. It seemed kind, giving, and easier. Their lives were busy, and I felt, after all, it was my job to see that the house ran smoothly. I know now that their busy little lives should have included consistent responsibility and work.

George and Caroline Valient of Harvard University conducted a study which verified the value of work. They found that (more than social class, family problems, or intelligence) a child's willingness and capacity to work was the most important factor in predicting his or her mental health as an adult.(1, see References, page 104.) Stan had been telling me this in various ways for years, but I always took it as a criticism of my mothering. He had maintained that it is *accomplishment* which makes people feel good about themselves. It had been hard for me to accept this message coming from Stan, because he had been a slave to accomplishment and he was a prime example of someone who did not feel good about himself. I now believe that Stan's drive and capacity for hard work are essential to his feeling worthy.

When I think about the handicaps that I created for my children, it is hard to forgive myself. I know how difficult it is for them to learn adult skills that have already become a habit to most children before they reach adulthood. It seems a strange paradox, but had I been a little more aware of my own needs and sometimes put them first, we all would have won.

9

A Matter of Self-Esteem

WHEN I WAS a child, my mother appeared perfect. She wasn't. As an adult, I realize that now. I thought at the time that she tackled all of her difficulties with ultimate strength and caring. I believed I could be like her and handle my life's problems with that same quality of perfection. *What I really believed was that my life would have no problems.*

I intended to have everything when I grew up—a successful, adoring husband, beautiful, obedient children, a "Better Homes and Gardens" house, perennial good health, and, most of all, the virtues of a saint.

This innocent belief was probably not too different from the hopes of many young girls. Believing that it is possible to live life flawlessly is a common fantasy of youth. Too often, this fantasy proves to be an impenetrable barrier to growth.

Many children are not encouraged to look at life realistically. I'm not referring to setting high standards or believing that one should strive to do great things. I'm referring to the unrealistic expectation that normal life is free of problems. While I was growing up, my friends and I considered the virtuous woman, the loving wife and mother, the ideal. Today's youth are more likely to envision a different type of perfection, but they are no better prepared to face adult life than we were. They are just being led through a different maze. Modern youth have cut their teeth on the fast-paced, multi-colored medium of television, which portrays everyone as beautiful, slim, and living the life of a Coca-Cola ad—fun and exciting. The model of the successful woman is now a "yuppie" who leads a busy social life while managing a brilliant professional career.

Now that our technological society has given us a window to the world, we can also view the *best* in every field. Our culture has come to idolize those who excel in the arts, sciences, politics, and athletics. We put them on ridiculously high pedestals and equate their special talents and attractiveness with personal worthiness. Constantly seeing those people with outstanding beauty and special gifts can make young people feel grossly inadequate.

It is doubly hard for the present crop of young people to deal with pimples, braces, knock-knees, fat, and immature talent while being bombarded daily with the beautiful and rich who live life from thrill to thrill in the fantasy world of television. Our society fosters the idea that each young woman should be beautiful, each young man an athlete, and that growing old is unseemly. Does anyone wonder that self-esteem is a monumental problem in our society?

A good many people have the added misfortune of coming from poorly functioning families, in which the parents not only don't actively work to build self-esteem but, indeed, foster a feeling of inferiority in their children. Developing a realistic view of life is crucial if one is to accept oneself as a worthy individual. No one can measure up to a standard that isn't authentic. Who among us can constantly be young, energetic, benevolent, and brilliant?

My childhood belief that I could have a perfect life and be an outstanding mother and wife served as a stumbling block to effective marriage and parenthood. Anything that transpired during our daily family interaction that did not fit my imaginary picture looked like failure to me. The farther my family's reality was from my naïve view of what it should be, the greater my loss of self-esteem. I erroneously believed that I could create the perfect home. When I couldn't create my fantasy, I felt incompetent.

Poor self-esteem is the principal factor in enabler-dependent relationships. Those of us who—for whatever reasons—feel unworthy, need to develop a realistic view of what human living is about. We need to discover the self-defeating attitudes we are still carrying around as a result of negative childhood experiences.

Since low self-esteem is at the heart of enabling, it is essential for enablers to reach into the dark corners of their minds and probe the feelings and beliefs they have about themselves if they wish to understand the sources of their behavior.

To understand the connection between low self-esteem and enabling, think again of Ray, who wouldn't allow his sons to do anything completely on their own—without Ray's expert advice. Ray's insistence on being the expert is more symptomatic of his poor self-esteem than of his great expertise. His own father, who is now in his seventies, still chuckles about the stupid things Ray did as a youth. He treats Ray as though he were a blundering boob. So Ray is passing the neurosis on to his sons—who will pass it on to their sons—ad nauseam. Unless someone in the chain has the insight and courage to alter it, the situation could continue indefinitely.

If Ray could distance himself enough to view his interaction with his sons objectively, I believe that he would understand the effect his enabling is producing. He then might try to discover why he feels a constant need to show his superiority. Ray needs to recognize his low self-esteem and identify its source. He could then allow his sons to learn to feel capable and independent, and he could also begin to do the things that would help him develop and enhance his own self-esteem. All Ray really wants is to feel good about himself and to prove to his sons that he is competent—since he will never be able to prove it to his own father.

When enablers look clearly at the factors that have contributed to their feelings of unworthiness, they will recognize that most of those feelings have been created as a result of the manipulation of others who likewise felt unworthy. Enablers need to learn how to replace the negative pictures of themselves that they have acquired, along with the deceptive myths about an ideal life.

Once an enabler begins to live a life based on realistic expectations and actual possibilities, he or she will find that *real life now* is much more rewarding than childhood fantasies ever were.

At the conclusion of this chapter and the next four chapters I have included worksheets of exercises which will be very useful to those readers who are attempting to overcome enabling behavior. Of course, working with a professional counselor or therapist is an essential part of any program to bring about changes in personal or family life. These exercises should not be considered a replacement for professional help.

Worksheet #1

Knowing Yourself

1. List all the qualities, good or bad, which you believe describe you; not what others have said, but what you in your heart believe. This should be a long list. For example: I am a female, tall, perfectionist, have a wide variety of interests, am the child of an alcoholic, get overly concerned about others, love to read, am a good cook, overeat, want everyone to like me, etc. Add to the list whenever you think of anything else which describes you.

2. Put a plus sign next to all the items that you *wouldn't want to change*, because they are positive traits; for example, I love to read. These are strengths—feel good about them!

3. Go over your list and star all of the things that *can't be changed*; for example, I am tall. Then, taking one item at a time, begin to *let it be OK* to have these qualities you can't change. Start with an item that is not overly threatening, and tell yourself several times each day that it is acceptable to be this way. Remind yourself that it is not realistic to expect yourself to be perfect or that the circumstances of your life can always be ideal. To be satisfied with yourself and your life, you have to willingly accept yourself as you really are.

4. Put all the items that are not starred—those that *can be changed* —on a new list, and keep it for use in a later exercise.

10

Committing to Change

LIVING HAS OFTEN been likened to a river, because the river is such an apt analogy of life's change and process. Most of us are constantly tumbling along, bending, narrowing when we must, widening when we can, but rushing in an ever-changing path to an unknown destination. In spite of life's constant flux, there are many people who become so rigidly attached to familiar things that their lives seem more like stagnant ponds.

Perhaps the most important difference between those who flow through life and those who stagnate is adaptability to change. People who live life in a fixed, well-defined territory suffer when any change or interference alters their circumstance. They are thrown into trauma when any significant unavoidable event forces a life change. Their energies are spent resisting the change, in an effort to protect what they have. (This is true even when they aren't at all sure that what they have is worth saving.)

I believe that the *ability* to change and the *willingness* to change are both important factors in living a satisfying and fulfilling life. I'm not alone in this opinion:

most psychological research bears this out. K. Warner Schaie of Pennsylvania State University has conducted a study of 2,000 adults, which correlates adjustment to change with mental alertness. He found higher mental acuity among the older members of the group who lived more flexible life-styles and adapted easily—that is, those who varied their routine and were open to new and additional activities. It appears that people who do not adapt well to changing situations are at greatest risk of losing their intellectual abilities.(2)

We all go through unavoidable changes that result from natural catastrophes, the death of loved ones, unemployment, illness, or accident. We all suffer from the loss of what once was, but we can grieve for the changes and gradually we will heal.

When enablers are forced by inescapable circumstances to give up the enabling position for a while, they are not really altering their enabling behavior—they are only on vacation. For example, if an enabler's alcoholic partner dies of cirrhosis of the liver, and there are no other relatives willing to fill the dependent role, the enabler does not lose his or her enabling character. He or she is simply between jobs while looking for another dependent.

Giving up enabling requires more than having the universe remove a dependent from your household. It requires a conscious decision to alter the way you interact with everyone, and particularly with people who slide easily into dependent roles.

This conscious decision to quit encouraging the dependency of others demands real commitment. Once you recognize yourself as an enabler and determine not to relate to people from a position of being needed, it is necessary to get out of the stagnant pond and go jump into the river. It is time to move, to be flexible, to grow, and to change.

* * *

Denial, however, can be a potent form of resistance. Refusing to see, believe, understand, and accept can protect a person from changing. Understanding, whether we like it or not, brings with it a certain amount of responsibility. Those who don't want to see or are afraid to look, simply don't want to be under obligation to act. Enablers who refuse to acknowledge their participation in co-dependent relationships cannot be helped, just as alcoholics who refuse to admit they are alcoholics cannot be helped.

Commitment to change is only possible for the enabler who has taken the important first step—that of identifying oneself as an enabler. The person who recognizes that he or she is an enabler will, in small ways, begin to change without conscious effort. Just this simple acknowledgment will trigger change, because the enabler has become open to a new understanding; it is too late for denial. I know that I will never again, with a clear conscience, be able to pretend such righteous indignation over my situation as I once could.

Recognizing that one is an enabler is one thing. Admitting it to others is quite another. The act of admitting our failures to those we have failed and attempting to rectify the damage precipitates a change in the way that our dependents respond to us—which causes us to respond differently to them—causing them to respond differently—and on the change goes. What we do is create a new form of interaction. Changing the format of our interaction influences the way others react to us, and this *has* to alter the outcome of the situation.

Bringing the issue of enabling out into the open interferes with the enabler's ability to influence his or her dependents' behavior. The jig is up. *When all of the parties involved in the game identify the enabler-depen-*

dent interaction for what it is, it loses its power.

Once enablers have made everyone else aware of the way they are behaving and the reasons behind it, continuing the behavior will make them feel foolish—a condition in which we enablers are accustomed to seeing our dependents, not ourselves. By clearing ourselves of past ways of acting, we open the way to a new set of responses. Since I made my public admission and promise of change, I am always nagged by my behavior when I slip into enabling. For me, enabling has been transformed from a behavior I used to feel righteous about to something which embarrasses me.

Breaking the enabling habit requires:

1. Recognition,

2. Admission of guilt, and

3. Commitment to alter that behavior.

I believe the first of these to be the most difficult. There is no way to force enablers to look at themselves honestly. The greatest resistance will be to disclosure. Once enablers see themselves for what they are, however, they will forever be impelled to change by the knowledge that there is a possibility of doing something about it.

In its ability to produce sweaty palms and heart palpitations, the word *commitment* is second only to the word *change*. When the two are combined, they can produce powerful resistance. Change is stressful to everyone. Moreover, commitment obligates us to constancy, a promise to be faithful and consistent in our actions. So committing to change can become a double threat, filled with ambiguity. It is an obligation to pursue the as-yet-unknown truths about life and about ourselves. Because of this double challenge, an enabler has to want to change. There are many effective techniques for cracking the enabling habit, but they are all useless until a fundamental commitment is made.

While commitments *are* serious, it is unfortunate that we have made them seem so deadly. The word itself has become synonymous with burden. To dedicate ourselves to a goal that will bring a greater fulfillment to us and to those who are special to us should be life-giving rather than deadening. When we choose to give up an enabler-dependent relationship for a mutually supportive one, it should be approached as a pleasurable challenge rather than a grim chore. It can be exhilarating, and it can bring excitement.

We all know, of course, why we are so afraid of commitment, and especially commitment to change. *We don't know what will happen should we begin something new, something that can't be reversed.* Good or bad, the present is known, and the known is secure. We have already accommodated to it. The wife of an alcoholic has the security of knowing that her husband will be spending his evenings passed out on the couch at home. Who knows what he would do if he became a fully functioning man? He might find another woman who has more creative ideas about how to spend an evening. That is threatening! It may feel safer for the wife not to do anything, even though she is miserable. The man who moans about taking his wife to parties because she clings to his arm and won't mingle knows that she will never stray very far. Should she improve her self-image, he will no longer be able to monitor her social contacts. He may worry about her loyalty should she make friends with more interesting people.

Enablers who commit themselves to developing self-fulfilling lives (that is, lives based on something besides having others need them) must be willing to face whatever happens to them as a result of their altered actions. They need to develop faith, to believe that they have the ability to create a rewarding life for themselves *under any conditions*. Accepting whatever happens as a result of the commitment to change one's behavior will give a person the courage to change. It is a matter of trusting that the universe will do its part, if we do ours.

Luckily, we are not required to live our entire lives at once. We live one day at a time. And that is the way our commitments should be tackled—one day at a time. Once we decide how we want to live, there is ample opportunity to practice. Each day is practice for the next. All we need to worry about is being responsible for the decision of the moment. Living moment by moment and having dominion over the moment can produce dramatic long-term changes in one's life. In moving through life, all we have to do is make a commitment to alter our direction very slightly, and then follow that course, in order to end up at a different— and healthier—destination.

Worksheet #2

Changing Yourself

1. Review the list you made for Worksheet #1, Item 4. This is the list of your characteristics which you identified as having the potential for being changed.

2. Decide which of these traits you would like to change, and think about *why* you would like them changed.

3. Choose one of the items on the list that seems to you to be the most simple to change and make a commitment to change it. Do not concern yourself yet about how you are going to accomplish the change—just make the commitment. (This worksheet is not adequate to help you attempt major changes—for that you should also have the guidance and support of a competent professional therapist.)

4. Tell someone you trust about this commitment. You may think that this is nobody's business, that you should make this commitment only to yourself, but research evidence indicates that people who make their goals public are much more likely to work to achieve them.(3) Social pressure keeps us honest with ourselves.

5. List three things that you can begin to do differently which will move you toward your goal. (Be realistic in making your choices—select changes that you can make successfully.) For example, if you are overweight you might decide to (1) eat smaller portions of food at each meal, (2) eliminate one dessert, (3) walk for twenty minutes each day.

Positive change, however slight, creates more positive possibilities.

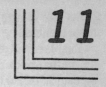

Facing Fear

WHEN ENABLERS MAKE the commitment to stop enabling, they step right into the middle of their personal fears. There is a real possibility that the altering of their behavior may represent the beginning of the end of a relationship. These warriors, who can firmly face everyone else's demons and fight with sword in hand to protect others, become paralyzed to take any steps when faced with their own demons.

The issue of personal esteem is so subtle, deep, and frightening to look at that most of us will not acknowledge it as a factor when we face the fear of losing a relationship.

Doubting our own worth is what makes most of us lose faith in the strength of our ties. Ideal ties between family members are based on love, respect, and shared goals. Feeling unworthy of our family's love can cause us to be afraid of losing their support. Making ourselves indispensable to our family members is an unfortunate but effective way of keeping them around when we are not sure whether they are with us out of love or necessity. Enablers' greatest fears are that their dependents will leave if they dissolve the dependencies they have created.

Enablers and dependents develop relationships based on mutual poor self-esteem. Each partner comes from a position of personal insecurity and counts on the other's insecurity to keep the relationship stable. Surprisingly, these relationships, while being grim or sometimes tempestuous and painful, are very stable—until one of the participants begins to work toward improving his or her self-image. When one or the other tries to break the cycle, the deep hidden fears and feelings of insecurity surface.

Neither party in the relationship may be willing to seek counseling because they fear that the only solution to their co-dependence is to dissolve the relationship. Separation is not usually the best answer. When partners separate without dealing with each person's underlying attitudes and insecurities, they will most likely re-create the same situation with new partners. They can be doubly demoralized and confused if they thought that changing partners was the answer, only to find themselves in the same type of relationship again.

It is not the relationship that is the culprit so much as it is the behavior within it. When both participants are willing to learn about themselves and alter the way they interact, their changed responses can precipitate growth in each other and alter the dynamics of their relationship. Making oneself happy *now*, in the present circumstance, is the real prize. It doesn't mean that either or both might not wish for "better" or "different" circumstances, but "better" or "different" are more likely to be created from a position of happiness.

When both the enabler and the dependent want to break their co-dependence, the chances are good that their bond will become stronger from their mutual commitment to improve themselves and their relationship.

When enablers are involved with hard-core game players, they may fear that their dependents truly only want a caretaker—that when they give up enabling, their partners will dump them for someone who will continue to take care of them. They may be right. I believe that the enablers' new self-esteem, gained in the process of working for a more rewarding life, will carry them through the loss and keep them from attracting the same sort of people to repeat their former co-dependent relationships.

The ability to distinguish a co-dependent relationship from one built on love, caring, and mutual work toward common goals is very important in understanding the dynamics of enabling.

Partners in a loving relationship are secure in the belief that they could survive separately. It is out of *love, not need*, that they choose to be together. Each needs the other only because they love the other. This is quite different from dependence, which is based on a feeling of deficiency and fear of being alone. In a loving relationship, the partners each serve as a cheering section for the other—knowing that the goal is to improve the quality of both of their lives. Combined, they form a dynamic unit. By contrast, co-dependents, while feigning support, are simply fostering needs.

These two types of partnerships look very different to a knowledgeable outside observer. To illustrate, I'll describe the situation of a wife, with grown children, who wants to return to college after many years.

A supportive husband would:

—tell his wife that she is capable
—offer to help with the household duties

—offer financial support
—not make her feel guilty for spending time on herself
—celebrate when she graduates.

The husband who wants to foster need would:

—tell his wife that he is worried that she can't com-
pete
—tell her that school is very difficult and that he
doesn't want her to be under that much stress
—tell her that she already has more to do than she
can handle
—begin creating more tasks for her to do around the
house
—make her feel guilty and inconsiderate for even
suggesting going back to school.

As another example, let me describe the situation of
a couple with young children. The wife who wishes to
support her husband as a partner in parenting will:

—show her husband how to feed and diaper the baby
—teach him all of the little tricks she has figured out
to keep the baby contented
—encourage special times for father and child to be
alone together.

The wife who wants to foster dependence of both the
father and baby will:

—avoid leaving the baby alone with its father
—withhold all of her knowledge so that she becomes
indispensable to both the father and the baby

—put herself in the middle, so they both need her
around as a go-between.

In these two examples, the principles are the same:
Each partner in a supportive relationship has high self-
esteem and believes himself or herself worthy of being
loved. They feel good about themselves and want to do
anything they can to help the other to feel like a worthy
individual. Enablers and dependents feel unworthy and
seek to bolster their poor self-images by standing on
the shoulders of their partners. They place the partners
in the position of being less rather than more. They
detract from their partner's already diminishing self-
respect. It is a downward spiral for both parties.

For those who have strong feelings of worthlessness,
attracting and keeping a mate and clinging to children,
parents, or friends is often an exercise in manipulating
the others into positions of need. Even the thought of
altering the "needing interaction" in such dependence
relationships produces a fear of losing the dependent.
Enablers are reluctant to commit to altering their behavior because they know that their relationships are
not soundly based on mutual respect.

There are many husbands who, with professions of
great love, bring home chocolates to their dieting wives.
Many wives, with loving kindness, cook oversized meals
for their overweight husbands—and then feel hurt if
their husbands don't show appreciation for their efforts
by eating everything. Once the underlying principles
are understood, it is easy to tell enabling behavior from
loving behavior.

Love relationships are based on one doing what is
best, *in the long run*, for the people one loves. Need
relationships are in fact self-centered, with the *pretense*
of concern for the partner.

* * *

Because of their secondary position in society, women are subject to even greater fears than men. Loss of a mate may represent loss of security, home, income, and status. A woman is likely to be programmed to believe that she needs a man, and she sets about to create a situation in which a man needs her. Should the enabler then want to change her relationship from an enabling one to a loving one, she has to face the possibility of losing both her emotional support and her economic protection.

While twentieth-century culture is slowly moving toward balancing the scale of sexual power, facing the problems of employment, housing, and safety in a "man's world" is a definite concern for women. For a woman to feel at the mercy of a male-dominated world is not an irrational fear.

I have often thought about my parents' relationship. As a child, I became very angry with my mother at times because I couldn't understand why she wouldn't leave my father when he was drinking. I see the situation differently now. She had six children during the Depression years. It was a time when it was not only difficult but almost impossible for a woman to obtain employment. Had she succeeded in finding a job, it would have paid very little. My mother's survival, and that of her children, was dependent on the farm that my father owned, and later, upon his rentals in the city. Taking care of him and picking up the ball when he dropped it had to be done in order to feed her children.

It would have been better for my father if she had let him fall on his face, so that he would learn to stay sober to avoid getting his face skinned. Had my mother let him suffer the consequences of his irresponsibility, however, my father could have lost his farm. That might have been a growth experience for him, but it would have been devastating for my mother and us children.

My mother, my sisters, my daughter and I have all experienced the frustration of not being able to exert direct power over our own lives—of having to check with the significant men in our lives to make important (and often unimportant) decisions. Over the centuries, women, not having direct power or influence, have resorted to cajoling, cunning manipulation, and subtle rewarding and punishing—all sorts of "behind the scenes" actions. Now that society is working toward giving us our own power, we are unskilled in using it, and we easily revert to the techniques of manipulation that seemed the only option for our mothers. It is time to stop judging *our* circumstances by those of our mothers and realize that in our society women have increasing power.

For a woman to break the pattern of enabling, she must give up trying to maintain control by manipulation and begin to exert the power that society is now offering. Women do, at last, have more choices.

Worksheet #3

Challenging Fear

Note: When trying to overcome a fear without professional help, it is best to begin with relatively innocuous fears. I am referring particularly to those which relate to enabling behavior. This worksheet is not sufficient to help you tackle your worst and most deep-seated fears—for those you also need the guidance and care of a competent professional therapist.

I have found that the best way for me to conquer fear is to dissect the fear so thoroughly that it loses its power to intimidate me. In order to dissect fear:

1. *Stop generalizing about the fear—be specific.* For example, if you are afraid to allow your son to miss school although he consistently misses the school bus, is it because you think he will get behind in his work? Is it because you fear being embarrassed by the school officials as a result of his absences? Is it because you believe he will enjoy being home and never want to go to school again? What are you afraid of?

2. If you don't understand why you have a specific fear, try to examine it closely enough to determine if it is justified. Perhaps your son is taking drugs most mornings on the way to school, in which case you have very serious cause for concern. If a fear is well-founded, it requires more complicated handling than what I'm suggesting here. Seek outside help.

3. Select a situation in which your unfounded fears cause you to behave in a manner which ultimately is detrimental to another person. (For example, because your son dawdles every morning and often misses his bus, you are now in the habit of driving him to school, thus rewarding and reinforcing his irresponsibility. You hate being a taxi service, but you are afraid of what will happen should he miss school.)

4. Decide what would be the best outcome *in the long run.* In this example, the long-term goal is for the child to become responsible for catching the bus every day.

5. Imagine all of the possibilities for disaster which could occur should you change the way you respond. Make a list of all of the worst things that could possibly happen as a result of his not being taken to school by you (he may miss school every day for the rest of the year, etc.).

6. Carry each horrible possibility a step further and ask yourself, what then? (He would get behind in school.)

7. Continue contemplating each new possible terrible thing that could happen as a result of your last answer, and project it on and on as far as you can go. (You would be summoned by the school officials— Then what? You would suffer the embarrassment of having to explain the situation—Then what? The school would send a truant officer after him—Then what? He would feel humiliated—Then what? Who knows? *Maybe he starts catching the bus!*)

If you dissect every fear and take it to its end, you will have adequate information to make an intelligent decision independent of the fear. You will also be able to separate the exaggerated fears from those about which you should be genuinely concerned.

12

A Question of Honesty

BEING A FRAUD is something I had always associated with being a criminal. But I began seeing the fraud in myself when I started looking more carefully at myself after the trauma of Johnny's illness. I began to see that the way I related to each one of my children involved some subtle form of dishonesty. I hadn't set out to deceive them any more than I had set out to deceive myself, and I am sure I was more effective at deceiving myself than them. But even the attempt at deception resulted in a barrier between me and my children that was difficult to penetrate until I finally quit enabling.

Not allowing my children to know how insecure I was at times, and how inadequate I felt in my job as a mother, was detrimental to them. Because I was uncertain of myself, I felt that I needed to be "right." The need to be "right" is a very insidious attitude, which often caused me to become caught up in a war which I felt I had to win. I would begin with the goal of trying to communicate with my children and end up embroiled in a struggle for victory.

My reluctance to "be wrong" built a wall between

us—a wall that didn't seem to have an opening through which they could reach me. And it doesn't take long for children to quit trying.

I know that there were occasions when my children needed advice and comfort but were reluctant to come to me because they felt that I wouldn't understand them. I see now that my children believed that I had only those noble thoughts and pure experiences I *pretended* to have. It is logical that they felt that I would have no basis for understanding them. They also believed that besides being misunderstood, they might possibly be condemned for having troubles. They were like many children who develop an unrealistic picture of the strength and infallibility of their parents. Children can feel so vulnerable and fearful when they approach an apparently omnipotent adult that they become discouraged from sharing.

I now realize that one of my greatest strengths is my humanness. Being fallible doesn't make me feel unworthy as it once did, but rather it gives me a certain contentment that I am at home with the rest of humanity. I am now finding that fallibility is my most powerful connecting link with others.

In the question of honesty, the problem of low self-esteem rears its ugly head again. A little digging usually reveals a deception to be the result of someone's attempt to save face. Most of us are very adept at communicating misinformation to others so that we appear better or different than we really are.

The hidden agenda is, "I may not be able to get out of you what I want, if you know the real scoop," or "You might think poorly of me if you really knew me." Unworthy people feel that they have to say all the "right things," whether true or untrue, to protect their position in life, which they secretly believe that they don't deserve. People with high self-esteem feel good about themselves and don't have to make up stories. If they make a mistake, their own sense of worthiness allows them to admit it—because they know that they are human anyway. Their worthiness is not based on how many mistakes they have made, but on the feeling that they are loved and respected for simply being themselves. People who are overly afraid of rejection, and capitulate to that fear, can never lead honest, straightforward lives. They do not have the freedom to be themselves and to say what they truly feel.

An enabler learns to be an enabler by being a pleaser as a child. An enabler develops the habit of keeping thoughts and desires secret for fear of reproach, anger, or rejection. Being this way, an enabler quite naturally has a distaste for, and fear of, confrontation and exposure. *To break the pattern of enabling, it is essential for the enabler to be honest and to say what he or she thinks and feels.*

Often only very trusted counselors are able to convince those with low self-esteem that it can be safe to expose their honest thoughts. But the therapists must first cut through their smokescreen.

After the incident of the tree, I began to be more honest and open with my husband about everything. I told him about feelings that I had kept buried for years. It gave me the most wonderful sense of relief. I had made an honest woman of myself. The biggest surprise for me, however, came from discovering that I hadn't told him anything he didn't already know. It seems that I had been much more successful at deceiving myself than protecting him.

"Putting your stuff out" is one of my close friends' ways of saying "communicate." I like this phrase because it is not loaded with the jargon that surrounds the word communication. The enabler can learn a lot from her co-dependent about putting her stuff out. When Stan was caught up in his own melodrama, he "let it all hang out." I became the tight-lipped juggler whose goal was to keep the situation concealed. I was adept at keeping my feelings and thoughts to myself. I did not want to be exposed as a less-than-perfect person, and I also tried to manipulate my family's environment to prevent their failings from being exposed. I felt that their flaws reflected on me.

I realize now that although my husband and John might have appeared more "flawed" than I did, they were at least much more honest.

Direct and open communication requires a strong sense of self-worth and a certain amount of fearlessness—neither of which enablers have. Enablers can display resentment at being misunderstood, knowing full well that they are the ones causing the misunderstanding. There is no way others can intelligently and caringly respond to us if they are led to make false assumptions as a result of being given false signals. When enablers won't let their thoughts be known, it is unfair of them to hold others responsible for misunderstanding.

Some enablers are so afraid of rejection that they will enlist a third party to "test the water." The third party's job is to determine if it is safe for honest communication. Unwary friends or family members often are caught between two people who refuse to talk directly. It is especially unfortunate when a child is used as an intermediary by parents who don't have the nerve to talk to each other. We have all used go-betweens and we have all been go-betweens. Our legal system functions through mediators. While mediators have their place, the relationship of enabler-dependent is an intimate one and will not become loving and supportive until the two people involved communicate honestly and *directly*.

Opening up and being honest is a wonderful gift to give a partner, children, or friends. The only way we can really be known is to allow others to know us.

Communication isn't always a two-way street. One party can be honest and straightforward in a relationship and still get back deception or manipulation. However, to break any established pattern of interaction, one of the parties has to take the initiative and be the first to begin speaking openly and truthfully. The truth is not only difficult to speak but it can be equally difficult to hear. If the truth is spoken with genuine respect and caring, however, it is a kindness which can serve as a foundation for the growth of both people.

Speaking honestly and openly can be habit-forming. I found that people responded with reciprocal honesty, and people who had previously avoided me started sharing with me instead. I had joined them in being human.

Being direct with a partner, when honesty has not been a customary part of the relationship, is very frightening. Your partner may have trouble with the truth, or worse, may tell you the truth about yourself. You must be just as open to hearing the truth as you are to speaking it.

Being honest actually helps overcome fear, and overcoming fear makes way for honesty. It takes both courage and faith in what you are doing to say what you think in a nonjudgmental way, hoping that it will be accepted with good will.

Worksheet #4

Speaking Honestly

In speaking honestly, *remember that your goal is not to win, but to establish communication.*

1. Make a list of friends and family members with whom you have misunderstandings. Start by making a list of two or three people, so as not to be overwhelmed.

2. Study each situation and decide what you need to do or say to clear up the misunderstanding.

3. Have no other goal than an honest intent for these people to understand you and for you to understand them. At your own pace, tell them, one at a time, that you care for them and want to remove any barriers which may have been caused by a misunderstanding.

4. Be prepared to listen to whatever it is they have to tell you, and be open to what they say. The scene from their point of view might hold many important truths that you need to consider.

5. Make a conscious effort never again to misrepresent yourself to others. If someone gets the wrong impression from what you say or do, quickly correct it.

13

Feelings vs. Responses

HAVE YOU EVER been told, "You shouldn't feel that way"? And you tried your best to do the impossible—not to feel the way you felt. The fact is that *one feels what one feels*!

People become very creative when attempting *not* to feel what they feel. They end up expressing their feelings in ways totally unrelated to the origin of the feeling. Psychologists have identified a number of strategies people use to stop feeling what they feel; these include suppression, denial, repression, projection, and displacement.

Suppressing an emotion is one of the most common responses to a difficult situation. One is aware of the unwanted emotion, but chooses to avoid or ignore how one is feeling. For instance, a wife who knows her husband is having an affair may feel hurt, but choose not to say anything about it because she feels she must maintain a stable home for her children. When the hurt overtakes her, she may ignore it by taking on activities to keep herself from thinking about it. Suppression, however, is only a temporary fix; until you deal with them, the feelings won't go away.

Denial is similar to suppression, in that the person knows what he or she is feeling. In this case, the choice is to insist that the issue and the resulting feelings do not exist. This is a very willful response: "I refuse to admit that this is real." For example, there are many people who can't admit they ever had feelings of resentment toward their parents. Very likely, they have convinced themselves of this. But we all have resented our parents at some time, for real or imagined wrongs. Simple denial can produce very serious problems. Yet it is possible to admit and overcome such resentments. We can discover the source of the emotion, analyze it, learn to forgive our parents, and go on with our lives. This simple denial of reality can produce serious emotional problems.

If a past event was particularly painful or threatening (for example, having been sexually abused), a person may *repress* that event so completely as to actually forget it ever happened. The incident, or even an entire period in one's life, can be forced out of consciousness, so that even if asked specifically about the issue, a person can honestly say that it never happened to them. It is possible to repress painful information before it has a chance to come to consciousness, so that one never experiences an emotion to begin with. Feelings left to work themselves out in the unconscious mind can become powerful and dangerous.

Believing that another person has the feelings we wish to avoid (while at the same time denying those very feelings in ourselves) is called *projection*. Have you ever known someone who claimed that a certain person disliked him, when it was apparent that it was your acquaintance who was doing the disliking? We often attribute our own feelings to others, accusing them of the negative or destructive emotions we feel. A woman who wants to leave her marriage, but is not able to admit these feelings to herself, may project them onto her husband. She may see infidelity written all over his face when he comes home late from the office, because that is what she would be doing if she were in his place. She may not love her husband any more and responds by projecting her feelings of disloyalty onto him. He, on the other hand, is devastated by her accusations because he trusts and loves her. He projects his trust and love onto her in the same way that she projects her discontent and disloyalty onto him.

Displacement means responding to the wrong person or object. If it is too dangerous or uncomfortable to respond directly to the source of a feeling, the response can be aimed at someone or something else. Getting rid of anger in an unrelated context, at an innocent recipient, is so common that the husband, angry with his boss, who comes home and kicks the dog is a cliché. Most abused wives and children are the victims of a husband or father's displaced anger. Researchers have found that an abuser is likely to have been the victim of the displaced anger of *his* father. He learned how to deal with anger by watching his father vent his feelings on the weak and innocent members of the family.

Enabling should also be on the list of destructive responses, although the enabler does damage in a more subtle and indirect way. Enablers allow their victims to harm *themselves*. They enable self-deception and self-punishment.

Strong feelings are almost always the excuse used by those who behave inappropriately. The abusive mother who strikes her son across the face can always excuse herself, saying—"I was angry." Actually, she was angry at her husband, but she lacks the courage to confront him so she hits her son instead. It may be true that her anger was the source of the blow, but feeling angry and striking a child are not the same thing. Anger is a feeling and striking is a response. The response is arbitrary. Feelings cannot be changed by force of will. How we *respond* to feelings, however, *can* be changed by force of will.

Any response is learned. With time, effort, and practice we can unlearn negative responses. A father who is upset from a bad day at the office may cool his anger by jogging around the block. Enablers can avoid sabotaging themselves and their families by acknowledging feelings and accurately identifying their source. They are then free to decide on an *appropriate* response, rather than giving way to an *automatic* response which may be misplaced and destructive.

There is also more and more evidence which suggests that altering seemingly insignificant behaviors has an effect on feelings and attitudes. Dr. Sara Snodgrass of Skidmore College studied the effects of modes of walking on the mood of the walker. She instructed some of the walkers in her study to take long purposeful strides. A second group was told to use a natural gait. The third group was told to shuffle along, looking downward. The mood of the first two groups remained stable, but the shufflers reported that they felt fatigued and depressed during their walk. Dr. Snodgrass' research seems to agree with earlier studies which indicate that taking on the *appearance* of a particular mood can indeed influence a person and bring about the thoughts and emotions associated with that mood.(4) Looking sad, for example, can produce a feeling of sadness. Acting angry can feed rage.

Obviously, there are many factors that contribute to the way we feel. Simply altering our behavior is not a complete answer, but it is part of the answer. Behavioral psychologists have shown that changing our behavior can affect our perceptions and beliefs, and these, in turn, are powerful conditioners of mood, self-image, and feelings. Feelings and responses, therefore, are reciprocal. Counseling gives us direction and insight; working to monitor our behavior gives us something to *do* and takes away our feeling of powerlessness.

Darby Prince and Peter Dowrick of the University of Alaska videotaped interviews with thirty-two women who were mildly to moderately depressed. Then they took the tapes of sixteen of these women and edited them down to only the shots in which the women were smiling and animated. All of their sad, depressive behavior was deleted. The women then watched themselves laughing and gesturing in these edited tapes. At the end of two weeks, the women who watched the tapes of themselves in a happy mood showed less depression than the remaining women, whose interviews were replayed unedited.(5)

Response is an important key to change! Changing physical patterns or routines can initiate different ways of feeling—which can initiate different ways of responding—and on it goes.

If you are an enabler or a dependent, you can make a conscious effort to retrain your responses. A professional counselor can help you with this retraining. Feel the way you feel—but *choose* your response. This is where your power to change lies.

Becoming involved in a co-dependent relationship is an unhealthy response to a feeling of low self-esteem. However, choosing a different, more appropriate response to these feelings can bring the partners higher self-esteem. Whether they realize it or not, they have chosen the way they react to the world and to each other. By changing their reactions constructively, they can initiate a thoroughgoing change in their life pattern.

Exercising a choice over how we respond to our conditions puts a great deal of control into our hands. Knowing that we can have control and exerting that control, however, are not the same thing. Psychologist Albert Ellis, founder of the Institute of Rational Emotive Therapy in New York, tried to determine why so many clients who seek help actually sabotage their own efforts toward self-improvement. After making a long list of the sources of client failure, he concluded that many of his clients opted for short-term goals, rather than sticking to a long-range plan which would serve them better.(6) For example, the woman who drives her son to school because he continues to miss the bus is sacrificing a *solution* to the problem in order to meet her short-term goal of getting the child to school *today*.

Responding immediately to a feeling, without concern for where that response may lead, is not controlling the response beneficially. The goal for an enabler is to separate the feeling from the response—not to deny the feeling but to gain control of where that feeling is leading.

Knowing and believing that there are things that we can do to change brings hope of new possibilities. And accepting that there are specific things about ourselves and our life circumstances which can't be changed gives us permission to quit struggling against them.

The prayer, written by Reinhold Niebuhr, used by Alcoholics Anonymous says it best: "God grant me the serenity to accept the things I cannot change, the courage to change the things I can, and the wisdom to know the difference."

It is hard to *be* anything but what you are, but you

can *act* differently than you do! *Because your behavior is part of the dynamic of your relationships*, if you alter your behavior in a positive way, your relationships *have* to improve.

═══════════════════════════════════

Worksheet #5

Responding Appropriately

1. Choose one situation in which you know your enabling is harmful. For example, calling the high school to cover for your son who ditches school regularly, or giving in to your two-year-old child when he throws a tantrum.

2. Study the situation and then determine the best solution *in the long run*. (For your son to quit ditching, or your daughter to quit throwing tantrums.)

3. Design a strategy to alter your behavior so that you can reach the long-range goal. (Perhaps you allow the school to punish your son, as they would anyone else's son whose parent didn't cover for him. Play calming music and read an engrossing book together so that you can live through your daughter's tantrums without giving in to her demands.)

4. Monitor your reactions day by day so you begin to do only those things which will achieve your long-range goal. Remember that change doesn't happen overnight. Keep practicing! That's what matters.

14

The Twelve Steps

MY FATHER HAD been an alcoholic, and I was determined to marry a man who would never abuse alcohol. So I married a man who was also raised in an alcoholic's household. My husband did not drink, but he suffered from recurring bouts of anxiety and depression. I had moved into a relationship very similar to the classic enabler-alcoholic type. After I married Stan, I thought his first depression and anxiety episode was simply the result of transitory circumstances. I was sure that if I were cheerful enough, helpful enough, accommodating enough, I could make him feel happy and secure—or I could alter the situation so that he would be happy. His periods of depression were episodic in the same fashion as my father's periodic drinking. My pattern of behavior was identical to that of the wife of an alcoholic. When my father went on a binge, my mother scurried around making everything "right." I did the same with Stan's depression.

When I finally recognized myself to be an enabling wife, I began to see that my enabling was not limited to my marriage; it permeated my other relationships as well. I was an enabler to other family members, friends, and especially to my children.

I also learned that the problem of enabling is much more common than I had supposed and is not limited to cases of substance abuse. It is unfortunate that almost all of the literature written to help enablers overcome their dependence relationships is associated with alcoholism. The literature, for the most part, ignores the large percentage of people who could profit from techniques developed by support groups like A.A., Al-Anon, and Adult Children of Alcoholics (A.C.A.). These groups don't exclude other enablers, but the enabler of a non-alcoholic dependent does not usually think to seek help from those dealing with substance abuse-based co-dependence.

The Twelve Steps of Al-Anon coincide with the Twelve Steps of A.A. and have proved extremely effective in helping enablers of alcoholics deal with their dependent relationships. Any enabler who feels responsible specifically for an alcoholic would profit by attending Al-Anon support groups and following the steps the organization has very carefully designed.

The Twelve Steps are:

1. We admitted we were powerless over alcohol—that our lives had become unmanageable.

2. Came to believe that a Power Greater than Ourselves could restore us to sanity.

3. Made a decision to turn our will and our lives over to the care of God *as we understood Him*.

4. Made a searching and fearless moral inventory of ourselves.

5. Admitted to God, to ourselves, and to another human being the exact nature of our wrongs.

6. Were entirely ready to have God remove all these defects of character.

7. Humbly asked Him to remove our shortcomings.

8. Made a list of all persons we had harmed, and became willing to make amends to them all.

9. Made direct amends to such people wherever possible, except when to do so would injure them or others.

10. Continued to take personal inventory and when we were wrong promptly admitted it.

11. Sought through prayer and meditation to improve our conscious contact with God *as we understood Him*, praying only for knowledge of His will for us and the power to carry that out.

12. Having had a spiritual awakening as a result of these steps, we tried to carry this message to others, and to practice these principles in all our affairs.

These general steps are useful to *any* enabler, and it is my hope that the public will become more aware of the effects of enabling in relationships other than those involving alcoholism. The world is full of people who are disabled because they were raised in "dysfunctional" families. They need a chance to get out from under the enabling of their caretaker, and their enabler needs to be relieved of the burdens.

I enabled my husband during his bouts with depression, and I enabled my children almost all the time. In fact, I enabled anybody who would give me half a chance.

Central to my enabling was the belief that I was *needed* to help others solve their problems. With my husband, it became very frustrating, because I could never solve his problems leading to depression. I learned at last that I could not make him feel any way he wasn't ready to feel. I began to understand that one person cannot motivate another. People do things for their own reasons—not for *my* reasons. I began to realize that others are not an extension of me and that they have a right to be whatever they choose—not what *I* choose.

I went through a series of transformational steps that were very similar to the Twelve Steps. I inadvertently took those initial steps outlined by A.A. when I finally decided I did not have the power to control either my son's illness or my husband's depression.

I have a friend who told me, after attending a meeting of Adult Children of Alcoholics, that he never wanted to go again because the meeting reminded him of a church service and he was an avowed atheist. I tried to explain that no one was attempting to force him to believe in anything he didn't want to believe. We discussed our beliefs about the meaning of life and death. He admitted that he did believe that there was some force in the universe greater than human power, even if it was the force of life creating life according to some universal law. I said, "That is the power greater than yourself that is referred to in the Twelve Steps. You don't have to believe in God in the traditional sense to turn yourself over to a universal power greater than you are."

Currently, there are secular support groups developing throughout the United States for those people who have difficulty with the religious overtones of A.A. and Al-Anon. The Secular Organizations for Sobriety (S.O.S.) is a friendly counterpart to A.A. and has evolved to meet the needs of those who respond to a different spiritual interpretation. The Twelve Steps, or any self-help measures, must resound with an individual's fundamental beliefs in order to be effective. It is essential to adapt each of the Twelve Steps to mesh with your personal ideology.

Many people believe that the great spiritual force of the universe is a divine power which resides within each individual, and that this power both constitutes and contributes to the universal scheme. In order to heal themselves, they must come to believe that this spiritual force, which they feel to be at the core of their being, will restore them to a more intelligent way of living, so they turn themselves over to it.

Hanging on a wall in my home, I have the "Desiderata." One phrase from it has always stuck in my mind, and I have repeated it to myself many times: "You are a child of the universe; no less than the trees and the stars, you have a right to be here. And whether or not it is clear to you, no doubt the universe is unfolding as it should."

When people believe that the universe is essentially good, they begin to believe that it is possible for the universe to take care of them and those they love. There is nothing wrong with asking the universe for one's share of the blessings, and expecting them.

Following another suggestion in the Twelve Steps, I made an assessment of myself (not my partner) and decided to bring my insecurities and my enabling out into the open. It seemed to be the only way I could break the pattern.

If we go to all the trouble and humiliation of admitting our faults publicly, we should be willing to accept whatever change comes as a result. This is when we need that special trust in the universe, because changing is difficult and frightening. We have to believe that if we change and grow, our lives will be better.

The next process in the Twelve Steps is making amends. I believe that asking forgiveness of others is extremely important—those we have offended will take our changing attitudes more seriously and are given an opportunity to respond differently to us. We open up a channel for some honest communication, and we also purge ourselves of burdensome guilt.

Before I began apologizing to everyone else, I apologized to myself for putting myself in such a ridiculous and demeaning position in the first place. Then I apologized to Stan for trying to solve his problems for him and trying to take over his life and choices. From there, I moved to my children, friends, and others. I wanted to be sure that all of my relationships were complete, so that if anyone I had offended died tomorrow I wouldn't be angry at myself for having left anything unsaid.

Because change is the essence of life, and is a lifelong process, I knew that all of the new practices I had started would trigger growth in me, and they have. I wasn't trying to reach a specific goal; I was trying to develop a different way of relating to people. I have to monitor myself continually so that I don't slide back into enabling. But every time I share my thoughts and beliefs about the importance of *leading a life which focuses on individual responsibility and honesty*, I recommit to a new way of being.

15

Living Differently

MANY PEOPLE PREFER trauma to indifference or
boredom. There is nothing more deadly to the spirit
than having nothing important to do or no one to be
concerned about. When trouble erupts in a household,
enablers have an opportunity to launch into action.
Trouble means added responsibilities for them, giving
them more to do. Trouble can mean upsetting interchanges between family members, allowing the enablers
to have more contact with each of them. Most important, trouble can bring the enabler a heightened feeling
of competence and self-esteem. Even the inner turmoil,
fear, and resentment the enabler feels is more rewarding than the blahs. There is something rather thrilling
to an enabler in the rush of adrenalin that comes from
being upset. For people who have forgotten the joy that
comes from an honest, direct, self-actualizing life, the
high drama of a problem brings a feeling of being alive.

For the dependents, creating tragedy or disturbance
helps them maintain the role and mystique of being
misunderstood. Sadness also has a certain glamour
about it. The pathos of unfulfilled longing can bring a

degree of pleasure which dependents are reluctant to surrender.

Both parties in a tragedy may enjoy the play too much to give it up. Or they may fear what seems worse: their own boredom, or indifference from those they care about. They cannot envision healthier options. One of the most difficult things enablers must do is give up the tragedy and trauma in their lives.

Unless enablers replace their dramatic life script with a more personally fulfilling one, they will find it hard to keep from spending time rescuing others from their troubles and responsibilities. Giving up an old habit is like giving up a worn pair of slippers. It is much easier to do when there is a new and better pair at hand. When the only apparent alternative is going barefoot, most people will hang on to their old pair. The key to successfully quitting enabling, after one has made a commitment to do so, is to exchange enabling for a style of living which is better and more rewarding.

Within the dynamics of an enabler-dependent relationship, it is the enabler who needs to start changing first. If the enabler waits for the dependent to take the first step, they may be waiting forever. Besides, we don't have actual control over anyone but ourselves. If we want change, we must initiate the process of change within ourselves.

An enabler can begin altering the structure of her enabling relationships by reassessing her obligations and duties within those relationships. She should return excess obligations and duties which she has assumed to their rightful owners, keeping only the ones that are legitimately hers. Since she will no longer have to mind everyone else's business, she will have much more time and energy for herself. Without the excuse of "too many responsibilities to others," she can now develop talents that she has neglected.

The reforming enabler should take time to really look at herself, taking an inventory of interests and talents which are uniquely hers. Once she has determined which among her many interests she wants to develop, it is time for her to launch a program of activity. She can be selfish about some of her choices because, in the long run, every individual's self-development works for the good of all. A good place to begin her program would be working with a counselor to get a better understanding of herself. (If she can have her partner or other family members in counseling with her, so much the better.)

Whatever she decides to do, it doesn't have to consume great amounts of time, but it does have to be her first priority. She can't let any family member pressure her to drop out of this activity. The new life must come first. If it is only dinner with a group of friends on Thursday evening, or an exercise class on Friday morning, she should let nothing interfere. She needs to start small, but start somewhere. She must begin to create an identity for herself and hang on.

Reforming enablers must not allow themselves to be intimidated or made to feel guilty about their projects. It is possible that, when they begin to spend more time on themselves and less on their dependents, their dependents will escalate their demands and exaggerate the inconvenience enablers are causing. The dependent is accustomed to being catered to and will try to maintain this position by sabotaging any plan or project the enabler starts.

Developing friends outside of the family or partnership will also help enablers to establish an individual identity. These friends will feed their personal growth and give the comfort of knowing that they have outside support to draw on should the enablers' relationships threaten to collapse. Friends will soften the fears.

As enablers' outside activities and interests grow, so will their self-esteem. They have to be secure in their belief that what they are doing is best for their dependents, and turn a deaf ear to complaints. Better yet, the enabler's own counseling may develop into family therapy, opening up an opportunity for each of the family members to grow and for family interaction to improve.

Beginning a new life based on realistic expectations and actual possibilities can look like an overwhelming undertaking, but it doesn't have to be. Slight changes in attitude and behavior make big differences. Therapy can help, as a source of insight, support and direction. Anyone who chooses to take the necessary steps to stop enabling others will find a happier and more fulfilled life.

Gradually altering yourself begins with:

1. Recognizing your own unproductive and self-destructive behavior (in this case, enabling).

2. Making a commitment to change that behavior.

3. Seeking to understand the sources of your unproductive behavior. Having a competent therapist at your side is the most effective way to begin a soul-searching journey. The source of many behaviors may not be visible to us.

4. Learning to face the fears that surface when a change is initiated.

5. Not accepting anything but loving honesty from yourself and others.

6. Responding appropriately to the needs of others.

7. Developing personal individuality based on your unique talents and interests.

To keep yourself from enabling:

Consider others:
  —Don't do anything for other people, including children, if they can and should be doing it for themselves.

  —Plan toward long-range goals to overcome your enabling situations.

  —Break your routine behavior by force of will.

  —Changing your routine will help change your situation.

  —Demand that everyone in your family contribute their fair share of work.

Consider yourself:
  —Treat yourself no worse than you would treat anyone else.

  —Learn to accept and forget the things you can't change.

  —Prioritize the things about yourself that you want to change. Start with whatever you decide needs attention first. For example, find a counselor to help with low self-esteem, or an assertiveness training class at your local community college to deal with shyness.

  —Cultivate the appearance of well-being and happiness. Take care of your clothes, your hair, your diet, and get exercise. Take loving care of yourself physically and spiritually.

—Make friends of your own. Don't rely on your partner or family friends. Join clubs, become a volunteer, take classes, get a part-time job—whatever it takes—to develop friends apart from your family or the dependent situation.

16

Love That Helps

CERTAINLY THERE ARE times when others genuinely need our help, care, and support. This makes it especially necessary for us to know how to make the distinction between help that makes someone stronger and help that fosters dependency. There is a difference between legitimate caring and co-dependent enabling. Children *do* get hurt, husbands *do* need encouraging, wives *do* need support, friends *do* need a listening ear. We all need help some time, and it is important to be available to others when we are needed. Enablers must learn when it is *appropriate* to help. Taking the time to think before jumping into a situation helps an enabler respond in ways that will not encourage dependency. When our "help" will prevent someone from learning something he or she needs to know, we should not rush in—because that is *not help*.

The particular configuration of my husband's and son's ordeals taught me that the predicaments of others are giving them valuable messages they need to receive. The help I was giving them only blocked the messages. By trying to remove obstacles for them, I had been taking away their right to solve their own problems.

Now when I'm confronted with a problem that is not mine, I tell myself not to interfere, that the problem needs to be solved by its owner. Since I started allowing others to tackle their own problems, I have been surprised by how ingenious and resilient they are.

When partners, children, parents, or friends have problems that are permanent, such as physical handicaps, it is even more important to allow them to come to terms with the situation as soon as possible, so that their chances of living life more fully are enhanced.

Enablers can begin altering the structure of their enabler-dependent relationships by reassessing their obligations and duties within those relationships. They should *return* all those obligations and duties which they have taken over to their rightful owners, keeping only the ones that are legitimately their own.

Breaking the enabling game is a real test of love, and love, like charity, begins at home. I am not referring to the home of the hearth, but of the heart. The love we have for others is directly proportional to the love we have for ourselves. It is because *our capacity to love is based on the quality of our self-love* that the pivotal point for helping those we love is taking care of ourselves, providing for our own growth, and developing our own talents.

Enabling behavior comes from not believing that we are intrinsically worthy. We don't have to be perfect, or superpeople, to justify our existence. It is our very fallibility that leaves us with directions to grow. What is there to learn if we already know everything? How does anyone improve on perfection?

Not hampered by our own insecurities and fears, we are able to more accurately assess the love we feel for others. While it might break our hearts to lose someone, if we can honestly look at him or her and say "I want you to be all you can, the best you can, with or without me," we know our love is genuine.

Enablers need to get off everyone else's case and get on their own. Leaving others to work toward their own rewards gives them the joy and self-esteem of accepting the consequences of their own feelings and actions. Enablers need to learn not to carry others, but to walk with them, hand in hand.

References

1. Cole, Diane, "Which Kids Succeed? Some Surprising News," *Family Weekly*, April 11, 1982, p. 7.

2. Meer, Jeff, "Mental Alertness and the Good Old Days," *Psychology Today*, March 1985, p. 5.

3. Stark, Elizabeth, "Tell It From the Mountain," *Psychology Today*, October 1985, p. 11.

4. Vandershaf, Sarah, "A Happy Pace," *Psychology Today*, January 1987, p. 68.

5. Meer, "Mental Alertness and the Good Old Days," p. 71.

6. Wood, Clive, "Their Own Worst Enemy," *Psychology Today*, February 1987, p. 18.

Suggested Reading

Adult Children of Alcoholics, Janet Geringer Woititz. Pompano Beach, FL: Health Communications, Inc., 1983.

This is a pioneering work which focuses on the common personality traits of adult children of alcoholics. It is extremely valuable reading for those raised in a home where there was alcohol abuse. Anyone raised in a dysfunctional family will find this book helpful.

Change: Principles of Problem Formation and Problem Resolution, Paul Watzlawick, John Weakland, and Richard Fisch. New York: W. W. Norton & Co. Inc., 1984.

Using set theory from mathematics as a model, the authors explain what forms of action are required to produce genuine, permanent change.

Codependent No More, Melody Beattie. New York: Harper & Row, Publishers, 1987.

A comprehensive handbook on co-dependence.

Getting Free: A Handbook for Women in Abusive Relationships, Ginny NiCarthy. Seattle: The Seal Press, 1982.

A useful and compassionate guide for those trying to release themselves from an abusive situation.

Love and Addiction, Stanton Peele with Archie Brodsky. New York: New American Library, 1976.

This book is helpful in understanding that many relationships are or can become addictive traps.

Marriage on the Rocks: Learning to Live with Yourself and an Alcoholic, Janet Geringer Woititz. Pompano Beach, FL: Health Communications, Inc., 1979.

Necessary reading for any co-dependent. If you or those in your relationships are not alcoholics, read it anyway. It provides excellent insight into co-dependency.

The Transparent Self, Sidney M. Jourard. New York: D. Van Nostrand Co., 1971.

An important book on the value of self-disclosure and its essential role in finding personal fulfillment and rewarding relationships.

Bibliography

Al-Anon. *Twelve Steps and Twelve Traditions*. New York: Al-Anon Family Group Headquarters, Inc., 1987.

Bandler, Richard and John Grinder. *Frogs into Princes*. Moab, UT: Real People Press, 1979.

Bandler, Richard and John Grinder. *Re-Framing*. Moab, UT: Real People Press, 1982.

Berger, John. *Ways of Seeing*. London: British Broadcasting Corp. and Penguin Books Limited, 1981.

Bower, Sharon Anthony and Gordon H. Bower. *Asserting Yourself: A Practical Guide for Positive Change*. Reading, MA: Addison-Wesley Publishing Co., 1976.

Branden, Nathaniel. *The Psychology of Self-Esteem*. New York: Bantam Books, 1971.

Burns, David D. *Feeling Good: The New Mood Therapy*. New York: New American Library, 1981.

Caplan, Paula. *The Myth of Women's Masochism*. New York: E. P. Dutton, 1985.

Cowan, Connell and Melvyn Kinder. *Smart Women, Foolish Choices: Finding the Right Men and Avoiding the Wrong Ones*. New York: Crown, 1985.

Dart, John. "Non-Believers Organizing Secular Version of Alcoholics Anonymous." *Los Angeles Times* II:6 (April 6, 1988).

Dowling, Colette. *The Cinderella Complex: Women's Hidden Fear of Independence*. New York: Summit Books, 1981.

Druck, Ken and James Simmons. *Secrets That Men Keep*. New York: Ballantine, 1987.

Fensterheim, Herbert and Jean Baer. *Don't Say Yes When You Want To Say No*. New York: Dell Publishing Co., Inc., 1975.

Fieve, Ronald. *Moodswing*. New York: Bantam Books, 1981.

Forward, Susan. *Men Who Hate Women and the Women Who Love Them*. New York: Bantam Books, 1986.

Friday, Nancy. *My Mother, Myself*. New York: Dell Publishing Co., Inc., 1979.

Glasser, William. *Reality Therapy*. New York: Perennial Library, Harper & Row, Publishers, 1975.

Harris, Thomas. *I'm OK—You're OK*. New York: Avon Books, 1973.

Keyes, Jr., Ken and Bruce (Tolly) Burkan. *How to Make Your Life Work or Why Aren't You Happy?* St. Mary, KY: Living Love Publications, 1977.

Kiley, Dan. *The Peter Pan Syndrome: Men Who Have Never Grown Up*. New York: Dodd, Mead, 1983.

Kopp, Sheldon B. *If You Meet The Buddha on the Road, Kill Him!* New York: Bantam Books, 1976.

Kopp, Sheldon B. *An End to Innocence: Facing Life Without Illusions*. New York: Bantam Books, 1978.

Lerner, Harriet Goldhor. *The Dance of Anger: A Woman's Guide to Changing the Patterns of Intimate Relationships*. New York: Harper & Row, Publishers, 1985.

Maslow, Abraham. *Toward a Psychology of Being*, 2nd ed. New York: D. Van Nostrand Co., 1968.

Meer, Jeff. "And the Depressed Feel Better." *Psychology Today* (July 1985).

Norwood, Robin. *Women Who Love Too Much: When You Keep Wishing and Hoping He'll Change*. New York: Pocket Books, Simon & Schuster, Inc., 1985.

Perls, Frederick S. *Gestalt Therapy Verbatim*. New York: Bantam Books, 1972.

Sanford, Linda Tschirhart and Mary Ellen Donovan. *Women and Self-Esteem: Understanding and Improving the Way We Think and Feel About Ourselves*. New York: Penguin Books, 1984.

Schaef, Anne Wilson. *Co-Dependence: Misunderstood—Mistreated*. New York: Harper & Row, Publishers, 1986.

Schmidt, Jerry A. *Help Yourself: A Guide to Self-Change*. Champaign, IL: Research Press Co., 1977.

Schneider, Jennifer P. *Back from Betrayal: Recovering from His Affairs*. New York: Harper & Row, Publishers, 1988.

Shapiro, David. *Neurotic Styles*. New York: Basic Books, Inc., 1965.

Shostrom, Everett L. *Man, the Manipulator*. New York: Bantam Books, 1968.

About the Author

Angelyn Miller, a professional in the field of human development and family relations, has had extensive training in Gestalt Therapy, Neuro-Linguistic Programming, Assertiveness Training and Transactional Analysis. Despite her background and training, however, Ms. Miller feels her personal experience in co-dependent relationships is her real qualification for writing THE ENABLER.